Diary of A Legionnaire

My Life in the French Foreign Legion

by

Gareth Carins

**Grosvenor House
Publishing Limited**

All rights reserved
Copyright © Gareth Carins, 2007

Gareth Carins is hereby identified as author of this
work in accordance with Section 77 of the Copyright, Designs
and Patents Act 1988

The book cover picture is copyright to Gareth Carins

This book is published by
Grosvenor House Publishing Ltd
28-30 High Street, Guildford, Surrey, GU1 3HY.
www.grosvenorhousepublishing.co.uk

This book is sold subject to the conditions that it shall not, by way of
trade or otherwise, be lent, resold, hired out or otherwise circulated
without the author's or publisher's prior consent in any form of binding or
cover other than that in which it is published and
without a similar condition including this condition being imposed
on the subsequent purchaser.

A CIP record for this book
is available from the British Library

ISBN 978-1-906210-39-7

Contents

Rouge

The seven-hour train journey from Paris to Marseilles seemed to flash by in a few short minutes. My mind was buzzing with endless reasons as to why I should just turn around and head for home, to the sanctuary of a stable job that my university degree would inevitably bring me. After all, no one apart from a good mate knew where I was or what I was planning on doing for the next five years. And apart from the usual preconceived images of funny white hats, forts in the desert and being buried up to your neck in sand, I knew very little about the French Foreign Legion. So why was I sitting on a train with a one way ticket, about to sign up to something I knew virtually nothing about?

Not surprisingly it's the first question that everyone ever asks me and it's always been one that I have felt a little uncomfortable answering. Probably because they always seem to have a look of expectation on their face of a dodgy past or failed relationship, followed by a look of disbelief and even disappointment when neither is forthcoming. It was also something that my mind was wrestling with as I sat on that train. I wanted to come up with a snappy answer that would make it all sound somehow normal. But I couldn't. The truth was, I liked the army, I liked hill walking, I liked travelling and I was looking for an adventure. So by the time we pulled into Lyon I thought to hell with it, that's a good enough reason for me.

I put my Walkman back on and tried to chill out for the last couple of hours with some decent music, and stared out of the window watching the French countryside passing by. It was 5th February 1996 and as usual on Sunday afternoons, the trains were quite full. There were two soldiers sitting opposite, dressed in their uniforms which looked incredibly old-fashioned. They wore long thick faded olive green overcoats, which looked like those old German numbers which had seen a bit of a revival in the 1980's with students, and their boots were a funny looking thing, half lace up and then a thick wrap-around buckle at the top. The jacket and trousers were cheap looking and didn't fit, and only minimal effort had been made to hold it all together with a loose webbing belt tied around the middle. Obviously France's main exports of chic and 'haute-couture' hadn't managed to get this far yet. Surely the French Foreign Legion being the elite of the French army, were going to be better equipped than these two misfits?

The train pulled into Marseille about 10 o'clock in the evening, and after toying with the idea of spending one last night on the town, I decided to head for the taxi rank and join the Legion straight away; my logic being that if I spent too much time thinking about what I was about to do, I might just talk myself out of it.

A cold Mediterranean wind bit into the side of my face as I made my way over to the Taxi rank and knocked on the driver's window. The taxi woman was in her mid sixties, had a cigarette hanging out the side of her mouth, and seemed the sort of person who could handle herself if anything kicked off.

'Legion Etrongere'

'La Légion Etrangère Monsieur'

'Qui'

Not bad I thought for my first French conversation. Mrs Strurrock, my old French teacher would have been proud of me. Anyway, we were on our way and with no way back I started to settle down and get quite excited about what the future might hold, because telling told this old woman where I was going had seemed to make it real, and I relaxed a bit.

We drove for about 15 minutes to a small town called Aubagne and as we drove up the hill, I could see what I had come for, the Headquarters of the French Foreign Legion.

I paid the old woman and walked up to the side gate, and as I did so I could smell the strong scent of pine forest in the air. It was dark, silent and there seemed to be no one at home. But as I stood there wondering whether or not it might be a good idea to come back in the morning, a Legionnaire stepped out of a shadow and greeted me with a rather unfriendly stare. Although he was wearing the same uniform as the two soldiers on the train, it struck me that he looked completely different. His clothes were pressed and they fitted him, there was a FAMAS assault rifle slung over his shoulder, and he wore the famous Legionnaires' 'white kepi', from beneath which he continued his icy stare.

'Legion Etrongere'

He opened the gate and motioned for me to enter. I followed him up some stairs into what was obviously the guardhouse which was dimly lit and heavy with cigarette smoke. Behind a desk sat a rather pissed-off looking bloke, who without saying a word got up and took my bag off me. He took a quick look up and down, before asking me if I spoke French. I said I didn't, and so he pointed at me to follow the guard I'd met at the gate. We walked in silence through the camp, which seemed to be deserted, as I suppose most army barracks do at 11 o'clock at night. But after five minutes we came to an old decrepit looking building, and after entering I was told to wait in the corridor while the guard went off looking for someone.

I could feel my heartbeat start to rise as I stood there alone, and then out from a side room came this really sour looking Legionnaire. Tall, lanky, pockmarked skin, sunken cheekbones and with a face of pure evil. As he stood there in silence, the guard turned and left. And as he did so, I felt my only lifeline leave with him.

After staring at me for a while, or trying to focus on me through the haze of his boozed up eyeballs, the sour looking Legionnaire came over and ripped my bag out of my hands and started to scream at me. My clothes and possessions where thrown everywhere as he just seemed to loose control. Completely confused, all I could think to do was to stand to attention and stare straight ahead. But after finishing with emptying the contents of my bag, he came over and without warning punched me in the back of the head.

He then started to drag at my jacket, which I took off, followed by the rest of my clothes until I was standing there in just my boxer shorts.

What the hell is going on here? I couldn't have pissed him off that much; all I'd asked was if I could join the Legion.

Alarm bells rang and I started to feel incredibly vulnerable. My hands were forced behind the back of my head as he paced around, shouting at the top of his voice. With him now standing behind me I was trying to second guess what was going to happen, when I felt a crippling punch to the kidneys which dropped me to the floor. Staying down I crawled into the inevitable hedgehog position in preparation for the onslaught of punches and kicks which followed, before I was dragged outside and made to stand to attention on a concrete slab with my nose pressed against the wall.

It was February, and within seconds my bare feet started to absorb the cold from the floor. In-between the shivering I tried to analyse what had just happened, but nothing seemed to make sense.

- Is this some short of initiation?
- Have I just been really unlucky?
- Or is he just some pissed up tosser who'd been bullied too much in the playground?

I don't know, and who cares, but after twenty minutes or so I hear the doors open and the Legionnaire's mingin' breath reaches me before he does. He grabs me by the neck and tells me to get dressed and pack my stuff.

Thirty seconds later and still not fast enough for him, I'm surprised to see the same guard from before appear in the door way and before I know where I am, we are again walking in silence through the camp towards the main gates. And on reaching the road, he turns to me and calmly says in broken English;

'Tomorrow 8 o'clock ici'

It was gone midnight by the time I'd started the short ten minute walk back into Aubagne. Angry and confused I tried to apply some kind of logic to what had just happened. As I wrestled with this thought I spotted a run down looking hotel, advertising rooms at 130 Francs a night. And so after paying out almost the last of my money, I pulled the chest of draws in front of the broken door, sat down on the bed and lit a fag.

I suddenly felt knackered as quite often you do when you've been on the go with your adrenaline racing, and then suddenly stop. I just sat there still a bit dazed and still not able to figure out of what had gone wrong. But whatever it was I wanted to know.

The problem with joining the Legion was that it was extremely difficult to get hold of any real up-to-date information that could answer the thousand and one questions I had. The internet was in its infancy in1996 and the Legion didn't exactly produce any glossy brochures or free telephone numbers, manned by multi-lingual recruiters willing to explain the HR package available and the terms of contract, along with your holiday entitlements. And the one thing that I did want to know about, was the brutal discipline that had become almost a byword for the training methods employed by the Legion. I don't think I was scared, or maybe I was a little, but I just wanted to know what to expect.

So far I'd spent only an hour in the Legion, had got the shit kicked out of me and been booted back out onto the street. But what I really wanted to know was whether this was representative or not.

Was the Legion really a modern professional fighting force? Or was it just a throwback to the harsh discipline, à la Beau Geste? Or was it simply a tough environment, filled with tough people, and in their world, this was how they did things?

One thing was certain; if I wanted to know the answer to any of these questions the only way of finding out would be to go back in the morning. Maybe naively, I convinced myself that getting a kicking was probably a one-off and that I would give it another go in the morning. I wanted to join the Legion and I wasn't going to come this far, just to turn around and go home with my tail between my legs, because of one bloke who thought he was a bit of a hard case after a few beers. Screw him I thought - I'm made of better stuff than that.

The next morning at 8 o'clock on the button, I was standing at the gates feeling as nervous and as apprehensive as I can ever recall feeling previously. As the Legion changed their guard at six every morning, I went through the same process as the night before and deciding not to complicate matters by explaining that this was my second attempt, soon found myself walking the same route through the camp.

In the daylight, it was a truly impressive place, and as I walked I looked down onto a huge parade ground which was centred with an enormous bronze globe surrounded by statues of Legionnaires. This I recognized from photos and had apparently been at the centre of the parade ground in Algeria. It had been painstakingly removed piece be piece and re-erected here in Aubagne, when the Legion had finally left their traditional desert homeland in the 1960's.

Following the guard into the same building as the night before, he opened a door to a room and gestured to me to enter, shutting the door behind me.

Inside there where grey steel bunk beds three storeys high and a number of stools, but not enough for the number of people in the room. The people inside were all dressed in civilian clothes and obviously potential recruits, so I made my way over to a spare bed and sat down. My first mistake was lighting a cigarette, which was like walking into a cage of lions and pulling a piece of meat out of my pocket.

'Cigaretta….Cigaretta'

Not really in a giving mood, I declined their most generous offer to smoke my cigarettes and ignored their responses…not that I understood a single word they spoke, but being sworn at sounds pretty much the same in any language.

From what I could make out almost all of the people in the room were Eastern European and seemed to be happily chatting away, as any group of friends might do with time on their hands.

A short while later, I was summoned to an office and started to give my personal details. My passport and wallet had been taken at the main gate but the corporal didn't seem interested in anything except filling in the blanks on the form he had in front of him. And after five minutes I was back with the other recruits and more than a little confused. No one had asked me why I wanted to join, or told me: That it was not like in the books. That five years was a long time and that if I was wise I would turn around and go home now….Nothing! All it seemed they wanted was my date of birth!

In the afternoon we were walked over to a compound that housed all the potential Legion recruits. This place was a melting pot for the fourteen recruiting posts from around the country and completely unlike any normal army recruiting centre. There were guys here old enough to be my father and they didn't exactly look as if they were in the peak of physical fitness. Others looked liked bikers with long hair and beards and the first thing that struck me was the distain with which they looked at us. There is a pecking order in the Legion based on length of service and it started here. We were as low as it got, still in our civvies until we were issued with minging green tracksuits, which in turn were exchanged for battered army uniforms if you were still here after a couple of weeks. At the top of the pile in the Centre are those that have gone 'rouge'. These are recruits who have been accepted into the Legion, have been issued with their new uniform and are waiting to go to Castelnaudary for basic training….or 'Instruction' as it was called here.

'Rouge' is what we all aspired to be. It was the first hurdle to get over and meant acceptance into the Foreign Legion. There were literally hundreds of people all chasing the few prized places and after a couple of unproductive days spent sitting around, I'd teamed up with an American who had joined on the same day as myself and a couple of English lads who'd already been here a week.

Bill was in his mid thirties, had already done five years in the Legion and had been out for eight. For his own reasons he was back and to our benefit he was a constant source of information and advice. Looking back, most of what he told us was utter bollocks. But he was pleasant enough, and at the time at least we felt as if we had a slight edge.

Dave was from the 'Valleys' and had spent five years in the Welsh Guards. Not particularly tall for a guardsman he had a solid, unflappable character and nothing much seemed to faze him. Quietly spoken, Dave was unimpressed with what he'd seen so far and was toying with the idea of jacking it in and going back to Wales.

Paul on the other hand, was from Texas and had served with the US Marines after they had paid for him to go to college. Loud, outspoken, fit as a butcher's dog and with what could only be described as a slightly insane streak, Paul was what you think of as a stereotypical six foot tall 'a man's gotta do what a man's gotta do' Texan. He always seemed like a fish out of water and during the swimming test, his own personal goal was just to beat any of the Russians.

'My name would be shit if I didn't beat them commy fuckers'

'Whatever Paul, it's a swimming test not *Rocky 4 – The Rematch*.....you've only got to do two lengths'

The days at Aubagne passed surprisingly slowly considering that we were trying to join the Foreign Legion, and every day seemed to merge into the next.

'Reveve' was at 4.00am followed by breakfast at five. Then a round of cleaning jobs known as 'Corvée' followed by entrance tests or free time before lunch at midday. There was more *corvée* after lunch, followed by more entrance tests or more free time before an evening meal around 5.00pm. The evening then consisted of a bit more *corvée*, which was then normally followed by an argument over what TV channel to watch. And as there were around 200 or so Legionnaire volunteers from every corner of the world, all crowded around an old TV set, the only compromise that ever seemed to work was to simply switch it off. But the final decision on this was always down to the TV Monitor, who was usually some brown nosing weasel type with 'little Hitler' syndrome. They obviously thought that volunteering to be in charge of the remote control would win them favour with the instructors and they took their job very seriously indeed. But for the majority of us, having to choose between old episodes of American daytime soaps dubbed into French, or watching French pop videos was no choice at all. But at least this took us to about 7.30pm, when we were herded back into our rooms for lights out at eight.

This may not have been too bad, but unfortunately there are so many people wanting to join the Legion, you only found yourself being tested a couple of hours a week. The rest of the free time was completely unproductive and was spent sitting around talking about the same bollocks you talked about the day before and chain smoking cheap French cigarettes.

Bill was constantly passing on his pearls of wisdom, and after the 53rd time of hearing 'Well, when I was in the Legion eight years ago....blah blah blah ....It wasn't like it is now you know .... blah blah blah ...Did I ever tell you about the time that the Colonel of the Regiment put a helicopter at my disposal ....blah blah blah ....', then getting a kicking on my first night didn't seem so bad.

Apparently the highlight of Bill's career had been during an exercise in Africa. When serving as a medic, the Colonel of the Regiment had put a helicopter at his disposal. Bill kept on telling us in great detail that if he had wanted to, he could have stopped the whole exercise if he thought things were getting too dangerous.

'It's not the Colonel who is the most powerful man in the regiment you know....it's the doctor....he is the only one who can over-rule him and the other thing ....'

Dave had been sitting listening and couldn't resist poking fun at Bill.

'Hey Bill, you're right about the doc being the most powerful man around. When I saw him yesterday for my medical, he told me to drop my pants, then grabbed hold of my bollocks in one hand, looked me straight in the eye and asked me if I liked making love to men'

'Yeah ....Well no one has grabbed my nuts since I've been here....how about you Gareth?'

'Na.... me neither Dave .....I reckon he must fancy you mate'

'Piss off will ya....I know you're winding me up'

Paul spotted one of the English speaking Croatians walking past and called out to him. 'Hey Buchy! Did the doc grab your nuts and ask you if you liked making love to men?'

'No....why?'

'See, told you Dave...it's just you man'

'Oh fuck off'

The truth was that we had all had our bits inspected and been asked if we were gay. But as long as Dave thought it was just him, then it was just too good an opportunity to take the piss.

9

By the end of week three, it seemed like I had been there forever but at least I'd successfully passed all the physical and mental tests. The latter had mainly consisted of drawing trees, which apparently was very revealing about your character and would dictate your career path over the next five years. There was also an interview known rather misleadingly as 'Gestapo', which was hyped up as being the make or break....An in depth interrogation, where the thumb screws would be turned in order to look for any weaknesses in your character.

For me that involved convincing the interviewer that I was serious about joining and that there was no need to change my identity as I was not in trouble with the Police. After which we chatted about a holiday I had recently spent in Malta and then I was told to sit in the corner and roll cigarettes. I didn't know whether this meant I had passed or failed, but I took my cigarette rolling skills as a very positive sign about my suitability to join.

The beginning of week four was judgement day. Either 'Rouge,' or a train journey home - and from the two hundred or so people who had joined in the same week as myself, we had been whittled down to around twenty. Most people had failed due to either the physical tests or the medical examinations, which seemed to account for many of the Eastern European lads due to the poor state of their teeth, something on which the French Army appeared particularly strict.

The twenty of us paraded first thing in the morning and waited to see if our names would be called out. It was rather like being picked for a football game in the playground, hoping that you wouldn't be the last one left. But in the end, 11 of us were selected to go forward for basic training and we were immediately doubled away into one of the classrooms.

Bill, Dave and Paul had made it along with Andre, a tall Italian who spoke Spanish, English and French. Buchy, another English speaker from Croatia had also made it, along with a Russian, a Hungarian, two French lads and a Tahitian called Towhowra. This then was our merry bunch and first on the agenda was the head shave. A 'zero' all over, and after that we were informed that the next five days before we went to Castelnaudary, would be incredibly busy. We had equipment to collect, documents to sign, work parties every day and two guard duties every night.

We were also politely informed that we were now no longer able to leave and that the holiday was over and the nightmare was about to begin!

After a hectic day collecting mountains of kit and trying to cram it all into two small kit bags, followed by cleaning the kitchens in the Sergeants' mess, we got back to our billet around ten in the evening, and set about ironing our kit and polishing our new boots in preparation for meeting two of our instructors who were coming the following day.

Unfortunately we'd only been given a single iron and the only electrical socket that worked was in a corridor on the next floor up. This helpful gesture meant that ironing our clothes involved carrying a table, a blanket and a clean sheet up two flights of stairs. So by the time we had all pressed our gear and I'd pulled a one hour guard duty, which consisted of standing outside the front door in the pouring rain, there wasn't much time for sleep before *revee* at 4 o'clock. But by 8 o'clock the next morning after having cleaned our room, the toilets and showers to within an inch of their lives, we were stood to attention outside in what we thought was a perfectly straight line, just as we'd been told to.

From the other side of the parade ground we could see two Legionnaires walking towards us and a whisper quickly passed down the line that these were our instructors. But more importantly they were from the 'Rep'. The 'Rep' is short for the 2nd Regiment Etrangere de Parachutistes, or the Legion's Elite Parachute Regiment, who even amongst other Legionnaires, have an almost mythical reputation as the toughest of all Regiments in the Legion. Fiercely proud of their history and traditions, they take only the very best recruits after basic training.

Whether this was actually true or not wasn't really relevant at the time. But what was relevant was that we believed it, and as they walked towards us I felt a very real sense of dread.

The one wearing the black kepi was Sergeant Heimer, a tall baby-faced Austrian who looked liked one of those annoyingly natural athletic types. If he ever decided to leave the Legion then I'm sure a career in Kays Catalogue would be waiting. But he peeled off and headed towards one of the offices, leaving the shorter, leaner and meaner looking one to come and introduce himself to us. This was Corporal Dias, seven years in the 2nd Rep and his first time as an instructor. Dias was Spanish and in contrast to Heimer, only looked about ten stone, was well under six foot and had eyes that darted about in all directions giving the impression that he was constantly aware of everything that was going on around him.

Without speaking he slowly paced up and down stopping in front of each of us in turn. He forced me to catch his gaze and staring at me it seemed as if he was trying to read my thoughts. I stared straight back not wanting to show any weakness and after a few seconds he glanced away and moved on down the line. And after going through the same ritual with all eleven of us and still without having said a word, he strode over and stopped in front of Pal.

Pal was Hungarian and looked unnaturally tall at over six and a half feet. I had first met him when I was cleaning the canteen earlier in the week. He had been going around the tables, pouring any spare sugar sachets he could lay his hands on into his mouth, banging on about needing more energy than most due to his height.

Whether it was because of this size I don't know, but Dias had seen something either he didn't like or could take advantage of in Pal; and without warning, punched him hard in the stomach dropping Pal to his knees and leaving him fighting for his breath.

Not that we were talking, but a silence seemed to descend upon us.

Dias it seemed had made a very clear point without uttering a single syllable.

After this warm welcome, the rest of the morning was spent with Dias screaming the same two phrases at us.

'Garde à vous!' Followed by 'Rapport!' Which were the commands for us to 'come to attention' and 'stand at ease.'

This was our first lesson in drill and any imperfections that were noticed by Dias, and there were many, were met by a psychotic stare and a punch to the sternum.

Unfortunately for us, the combat jackets we wore had a Velcro patch conveniently placed in the centre of the chest where you would normally wear your rank. But as we didn't have any yet, this doubled up as a perfect aiming point for Dias, thereby ensuring that each punch was more painful than the previous one as it always landed in the same spot.

After lunch, which was followed by more corvée in the Sergeants' mess, Sgt Heimer who had not spoken to us before explained the reason behind our impromptu drill lesson.

Although we had already signed the five-year contract on the day we arrived, we had not yet been formally accepted into the ranks of the Legion. And this ceremony was going to take place this afternoon, in the tomb of the Legion's most famous son - Capitaine Danjou, who had been killed in Mexico at the battle of Camerone on 30th April 1863. His wooden hand, which had been recovered after the battle, forms the centrepiece to a sectioned-off part of the Legion's museum at Aubagne. Surrounding this shrine on large placards hung on the walls are the names of every single Legionnaire to have been killed in action since its formation in 1831. And if ever you needed a reminder of the type of unit you were about to join, then for me, this was it.

It was here that we formed up in a U-shape around the room, with Heimer and Dias positioned in the middle facing out. The room was decorated with grand paintings and artefacts from wars gone by, and for a moment I tried to enjoy the serenity and peacefulness of the place. This was probably the first quiet moment I could remember in the last four weeks, but the silence was abruptly shattered by Heimer's screeching voice.

'GARDE A VOUS!'

We sprang to attention as one unit, or as close to one unit as you could expect after only a couple of hours' worth of Dais's

intensive drill course, with our hands by our sides and fingers pointing towards the floor just as we had been taught, (not like the
clenched fist as in the British Army), our chins up and staring
straight ahead.

From the corner of my eye I could see the General enter the
room. This was the COMLE, or the commanding officer of the
whole Foreign Legion and this was normally the only time that we
would see him during our service. Unless, that is, we managed to
make it to the end of our contract, which for every Legionnaire,
irrespective of rank or length of service, ended here, once again
back in the tomb of Capitaine Danjou being addressed by the
General….\just as it was about to begin for us.

There was a real sense of occasion created in that room; that
this was the start of something incredibly important for all of us.
Whatever our previous circumstances had been or our reasons for
coming to find the Legion, that didn't matter any more. We all now
had a clean slate, and by comparison the previous three weeks
seemed as if we had just been going through the motions: filling in
forms, running around athletic tracks, putting ticks in boxes etc.,
until we had amassed enough ticks to be accepted.

As the General spoke to us (none of which I understood), I
wondered whether I would be one of those back here in five years,
listening, and this time understanding. And how many of the faces
around the room would be there with me? Would Bill be
there…..still bullshitting probably, to anyone who would listen?
Would Paul have gotten over his obsession with proving that he as
an American had to be better than any of the Russians? Would
Dave be there? Andre? Buchy?

February 2001 seemed an awfully long way off.

The rest of our week at Aubagne was spent being kept as busy as
possible with cleaning jobs most days, either in the kitchens of the
Officers' or Sergeants' messes. These would always run late into
the evenings and would be followed by pointless guard duties,
which always ensured that we didn't get much sleep and woke
every morning absolutely knackered.

Heimer was rarely seen and Dias was still a man of few words; but just kept hinting that we were filling time here until the end of the week, when we would be getting the train to Castelnaudary where he could really start to put us through our paces. Whilst at Aubagne he explained, he was not allowed to punish us too severely as there were too many officers about. But once we had started training for real at the 'Farm', then he would have no one to answer to and we would see what being a Legionnaire really meant.

In anticipation I rubbed my chest bone, which was still bruised from our first drill lesson, and wondered what he meant. But although a little apprehensive, I was looking forward to getting out into the hills to start basic training and leaving behind the pots and pans of the kitchens, to the next lot of Legionnaire hopefuls who would be going 'rouge' in a couple of days' time. It seemed as though we spent 95% of our time cleaning stuff, and that usually meant cleaning someone else's stuff; all of the time being overseen by some fat grumpy bastard who was coming to the end of their twenty-year service and had found themselves put in charge of the corvée team in one of the kitchens.

Whatever the future might hold for us, I would be glad to get away from Aubagne and hand over the baton.

We waited in silence on the platform for our train to Castelnaudary and must have made a humorous sight for the civilians passing by. Heimer was off sorting out the tickets and Dias as usual was standing in silence, with us in a line behind him, each wearing our new combat uniform and with two canvas stuff bags at our feet. For head dress we wore the Legion beret, but with a different cap badge that identified us as the lowest form of military life. The famous white kepi and the rank of Legionnaire would only be awarded if we survived a gruelling month spent at the 'Farm.'

As the train pulled in, Dias motioned for us to board and although we had only been together for a few days and couldn't really converse with each other, we were already starting to work as a team. So without waiting to be told, we automatically formed a chain and started loading our kit.

The carriage was one of the old fashioned types, being spilt into separate compartments which sat six and contrasted the modern TGV that I'd caught from Paris. Our journey was to take us the best part of four hours, but we were not allowed to go to the buffet car or speak to any civilians. And if we wanted to go to the toilet then we were to inform Dias who was in the next compartment.

In our compartment were Bill, Dave, Paul, Buchy and Andre. Given that we had the next four hours to ourselves with nothing to do, which was a rarity in our circumstance, we sat back and chatted.

Andre was originally from Milan and was well educated, speaking a host of languages, which meant he was one of the few that could converse with most people in our group. This, along with his likeable character and good performances on the running track during the assessments had already identified him as one of the stronger volunteers. Now in his late twenties, he had for the past five years been working in Los Angeles as a driver and gardener for Versace, living in his mansion and driving the occasional Hollywood star around in between doing the school run. Bored with life and seeking adventure, Andre had left Hollywood to join the Legion and couldn't wait to start soldiering.

Buchy was in his mid twenties and had fought in the Balkan War as part of an artillery regiment. Wanting to leave home after the war for a better life, he had taught himself English by watching American sitcoms which were shown on television with Croatian subtitles. And although a bit of a brown noser and the self professed expert on everything, he was likeable enough and had a harmless character.

Our talk inevitably turned to what awaited us at Castel. Given Dais's brief insight, our impressions were not good, but we all agreed that it would be easier if we stuck together and worked as a team. Andre had heard from one of the French lads that we would be made to run from the train station to the camp with all our kit, and as we did not know how far it was, we made plans that we would split into pairs. Each of us would sling one of the stuff bags across our shoulders and the remaining two bags we would stack on top of one another and carry between us like a giant suitcase. This way we could at least carry all of our bags and still be able to swap arms once they got tired.

Pleased with our little plan, the conversation slowly died away as we all turned to our own thoughts. The rarity and importance of a respite like this was not lost on any of us, and we all wanted to savour each single second and squeeze every last drop out of it before we pulled into Castel.

The train started to slow down a few miles before the station and we began to get ourselves together in anticipation of the run to camp. We threw water down our necks; made sure our boots were tied properly and ensured that our uniforms were comfortable.

Paul, who had his head crammed out of the small window in the carriage, shouted that he could see the station approaching and we all stood up, eager to get off the train and get going.

'Just remember....Stick together and don't leave anyone behind'

By the time the train stopped, Dias was already on the platform and shouting at us to hurry up and unload our gear.

It was slung onto the platform as quickly as we could manage and in a matter of seconds we'd disembarked and were formed up in a line, awaiting our next command. But in typical Dias fashion it didn't come and so marching off at the quick pace, we instinctively picked up our bags and followed him in single file out of the station.

'Right lads this is it....whatever happens, just keep going and don't stop'

Dave's words were calming, but the tension was still rising in anticipation of the coming run in our new boots and at this stage I just wanted to get going. I'd trained hard before coming to the Legion, running most nights and training once a week with a rucksack on, so I was confident that I would not make a complete arse of myself.

As we waited for the command to start running, an army truck pulled up and Dias motioned in silence for us to get on. We looked in puzzlement at one another as we clambered in the back and sat on the benches that ran down the length of the truck. Was this some cruel trick? Were we going to get on and then be told to get off and follow on foot?

After ensuring we were all loaded on, Dias mounted last and the driver closed the tail gate behind him. Picking up on our confusion, he sat down and lit a cigarette.

'What....Did you think you were going to have to run?.... Maybe next time'

Castel

One of the first things that stuck me about Castel, or Quartier Capitaine Danjou to give it its official title, was the size of the place and how new it looked. By comparison to parts of the camp in Aubagne which were made up of old-looking concrete buildings, most of which were in need of replacing, this place looked like it had only just been built. And in a bizarre way, I found the modernisation of the place strangely comforting. My thirst for knowledge of what exactly I was trying to join was insatiable, and so little things like the newness of the buildings were the only clues I had to piece together. Modern buildings might mean that the Legion was a modern Western European army, and that all the horror stories had been left in the past. A crude connection to make I know, but at the time it's all I had to go on.

We knew the camp itself was the main training establishment for the Foreign Legion, which included the raw recruits like us, but also Legionnaires who were undergoing specialist training to become radio operators, medics or mechanics, and it also housed those who were hoping to become corporals and sergeants. As such there were fantastic training facilities here, which included running tracks, swimming pools, indoor firing ranges that electronically noted where your rounds had hit the target, and an enormous amount of support staff to ensure the whole thing kept ticking over. Immaculately kept, the camp had been built on this new site to replace the old barracks in town which were starting to crumble away and were becoming too small.

Situated on the edge of the Canal Du Midi, located a few miles outside the town of Castelnaudary, the camp's main features were its two large parade squares, each one being surrounded by four accommodation blocks. These housed a company of Legionnaires each and it was outside one of these that our truck stopped.

Dias was out within seconds, not bothering to wait for the driver to drop the tailgate but opting instead to vault over the side. He started shouting at us to follow and unload our gear at the double, and before the driver was even out of the cab, we were formed up in two ranks in what was already becoming second nature.

Waiting for us on the hard standing was another corporal, Dabka, who was from the Czech Republic and had been in the Legion for three years, having served all his time in French Guyana, splitting his time between guarding the European space programme and specialising in jungle warfare. He was to be our second training corporal and along with Dias would be responsible for our day to day life.

The pace had notably increased since leaving Aubagne and everything seemed to be happening at 100 miles per hour. And so after sprinting upstairs and dumping our stuff, we were given ten seconds to form up back downstairs. This we failed to achieve before Dias had finished counting out loud and our punishment was twenty five press ups. These we had to number off in French, so that it also doubled up as our first language lesson. But unfortunately counting to ten was just about my limit, so I tried making similar sounds to the French speakers and hoped no would notice. Dias also told us that as we hadn't been taught how to march yet we would have to run everywhere, and so after getting our own guided tour of the quartier at the double, by way of the 'scenic route', we eventually ended up at the cookhouse, where we were given just enough time to throw down our food before Dias was motioning for us form up outside.

Here, whilst waiting for Dias, I saw a group of Legionnaires marching towards us. It was the first time I'd seen a unit of the Legion marching and it was an incredible sight, totally unlike any other group of marching soldiers I'd ever seen. Their pace was an eerie 88 steps per minute, which was only just a bit quicker than a funeral march and they were singing a slow melancholy song which echoed around the parade square, creating a sombre atmosphere and helping to ensure that their pace never altered. The hairs on the back of my neck stood up and even though I could not understand the words, it was a truly impressive sound. I didn't join the Legion to march and sing, but if I was going to have to, then I would be proud to do it like this.

Back in our rooms that evening we were given a brief by Dias. We would only be spending the next day in Castel because we were going straight to 'The Farm'.

Normally we would have to wait for another group to join us from Aubagne to boost our numbers, but it had been decided that although we were only eleven, we would be trained as one unit. The word 'farm' wasn't something that normally drove fear into the hearts of grown men, but the mere mention of the word here had most of us questioning our own motives for joining the Legion. I don't know why, but probably sparked by some primeval fear of the unknown that we all have. Not having any knowledge of the facts, our minds were being left to fill in the blanks, and as none of the things being said about the place were good, it wasn't something any of us were looking forward to. And what I could not understand was why we needed to leave the training camp for the first month anyway. What were we going to do at the 'Farm,' which we could not do here?

Bill explained that in his day, the 'farm' was used as a way of breaking you down. Your individual instructors decided on the best way to do that, and it was up to them to decide how hard things were. Hence, there was no real continuity about it, because as long as we learnt the basics of drill and a few other things, the rest of the training programme was entirely down to the instructors. This not only worried me, but it also confused me. To my mind basic training in any army should be a well organised and structured affair, where every recruit goes through the same programme and is trained to the same standard irrelevant of whom the instructors might be. A system that relied entirely on what the instructors thought was important to know and how to best to teach it seemed like madness. But then I guess that the Legion doesn't see itself as just 'any' army, and although I was not looking forward to the 'farm' I was looking forward to starting basic training, and there was a prize at the end of the 'farm' that I definitely wanted. I knew that we would march each week, with the distances increasing each time and culminating in a two-day 80 – 100 kilometre march, depending on the instructor's discretion and the route taken. This was called the 'Marche Kepi Blanc,' and if we made it to the end we would be awarded the illusive white Kepi and the prized rank of Legionnaire. For me, this is what I wanted and would hopefully keep me motivated over the next month. And as Bill kept on saying…. 'Once you've got that Kepi on your head, no one can ever take it off you again.'

Later that same evening after being assigned rooms, we were given tasks and paired up with our 'bi-nome'. This was a French speaker who was paired up with a non French speaker and would ensure that every order was understood. I was placed with Didier, a Frenchman who had been a sergeant in the French army and had decided to jack it in to join the Legion. Didier was literally going to be my ears all the way through basic training, and as a pair we would look after one another.

Didier looked like Smeegle from Lord of the Rings and although intelligent and a great runner, was altogether a bit too serious for me and came across as a little bit smug and superior. Occasionally a likeable bloke, he would hopefully teach me French before I left Castel and in return, I would hopefully be able to teach him a sense of humour.

Either way, if we both wanted to get through 'the farm' we would have to come to trust and rely on each other.

As the truck pulled out of the main gate from Castel a day later, I felt that I was able to catch my breath for the first time. I sank back into the bench and tried to enjoy the view as we sped along country roads and through deserted towns. The canvas sides of the truck had been rolled up and we sat back to back on the benches that faced outwards. The temperature was cool, but with the sun shining bright, the journey was pleasant and enjoyable. The past two days had been none stop with loading trucks and collecting the equipment that we would need for the next month, but at least whilst in transit there was nothing for us to do except chat and enjoy the rest. It almost felt like being a child again, getting all excited about a day trip out in the car. Unfortunately though I don't think our end destination involved hot dogs and ice cream, but there was a good atmosphere on the truck, as we felt like soldiers for the first time….even if we did know next to nothing and were driving into the unknown.

The towns began to give way to villages as we started to climb higher into the foothills of the Pyrenees and the engine started to whine more as it was forced to drop down through the gears to prevent us from stalling. A gear miss meant we were all jolted backwards, sliding down the benches and landing on Dias, which resulted in him hurling abuse; what he was going to do to the driver if it happened again.

Bill was in good spirits and I could hear him bending Didier's ear about some past glory and how the next month would be tough, but he had done it once before and so could easily do it again. It sounded more like he was trying to convince himself, as Bill had told me when I'd first met him in Aubagne, that as an ex-Legionnaire he would only be with us for a short while before he would be accepted straight back in. He was pissed off about having to do basic training again, but I also got the sense that he was more than a little worried. Bill knew how hard the next month was going to be and at 34 he was carrying a few too many pounds.

Although at times a bit of a bullshitter, I genuinely admired the hell out of Bill. Coming back here and doing this all over again took courage, and whatever else he may have been, he certainly had some bollocks.

As the temperature dropped and I was starting to wish they had let us wear our warm parka jackets, the truck slowed as it turned off the road onto an unmade track and came to a stop.

'RASSEMBLEMENT
DEPECHEZ VOUS
DIX, NEUF,….
AVEC SAC A DOS….TETE DE NEU

HUIT , SEPT....
ALLEZ ALLEZ'

Before we'd had time to sort ourselves out, Dias had already set off up the hill at a gallop, and throwing our rucksacks on we tried in vain to keep up. I could hear Dabka at the back somewhere shouting abuse at the slower ones, and after only 100 meters or so there were gaps in the ranks as people started to fall behind. We entered through the gates of the 'Farm' and quickly forming into two ranks, were made to do press ups, still with our rucksacks on, until the last of our group arrived.

Bill, who arrived second to last, was met with a stare and a knowing look from Dias. A sort of 'I respect the fact that you've been here before....but don't take the fucking piss.'

Pal, who was last, received a slightly less subtle punch to the sternum that knocked him backwards.

'Garde à vous!'

We snapped to attention with Dias and Dabka by our side.

Dias saluted Sergeant Heimer, who in turn, stood us at ease and then immediately called us to attention again.

Heimer turned and saluted someone we'd not seen before, who introduced himself as Adjutant Pinto, our platoon commander for basic training.

Adjutant is the equivalent rank of Sergeant Major in the British Army, or the highest ranking non-commissioned officer, which meant that he had started out in life as a Legionnaire and worked his way up. Pinto was short and agile, with a tanned weathered face that made it difficult to tell his age. He constantly moved while he spoke, gesturing all the time with wild arm movements and I could not help but notice, that his black kepi squashed down on his little head looked slightly comical

With Didier doing his best to translate, Pinto told us that physical fitness was his thing and that the next month would test us all to our limits and then beyond. We would learn what our bodies were physically capable of and he did not expect all of us to make it. We would run every day, do two night marches a week and learn the basics of combat and shooting. In addition we would also learn to sing and march like Legionnaires. Our own language was now forbidden and learning French would be a priority.

One of the things I'd noticed since being here was that I'd seen very few Officers. Most of the interviews at Aubagne had been conducted by sergeants and our only contact with officers had been with the General, and I was quietly hoping for a Lieutenant as a platoon commander. I don't know why! I just thought that it might balance things out a bit.

Anyway, Pinto it was, and at first impressions apart from seeming as mad as a fucking hatter, he appeared an honest and straightforward sort of bloke.

We were given a brief tour of the 'Farm', and what a shit hole it was. Even the most ruthless estate agent would be hard pressed to sell the qualities of this place. It was located on the side of a shallow valley and set on two floors. The upstairs was our sleeping accommodation and consisted of knackered bunk beds with damp mattresses, and a battered grey steel locker each. The wash room was one long cast iron trough with a couple of cold-water taps, but the selling point of the whole place were the showering facilities. The bank of four showers only had ice cold water, which considering we were at the base of the Pyrenees and it was only March, would mean that getting a shower would be more of a punishment than a way of washing.

By the time we had unloaded the trucks at breakneck speed it was time for dinner. But only after a little *aperitif*, which involved climbing a five-metre rope using only your arms. Those who could not make it were made to do press-ups to increase their upper body strength; and for those who were deemed not to be putting in enough effort, a Dias punch was also awarded as a form of motivation.

Most us managed to make it to the top, even though the cold air made the nylon rope bite into our hands, but Paul, despite being a good runner, surprisingly found it difficult. But it was Towhowra, built like a prop forward, who was the funniest. After a gargantuan effort making it almost to the top, which seemed to take forever and mainly consisted of grunting noises and huge farts, his grip gave way and he ended up in a heap on the floor.

I think Dias wanted to laugh, but instead maintained his usual stony face and ordered him back in line.

Repas de Soir, was as military an affair as everything else in the Legion. We stood and waited with our meagre portions of food in front of us, drooling like Labradors being teased with titbits. We would come to attention when the Adjutant entered the room and sit down on his command.

Bon appetit!!

Merci mon Adjutant....this was our cue to shovel the food down as quickly as possible, which normally took us less than a minute. The meal, which consisted of a piece of bread and a plate of tinned beans, was next to nothing and in no way made up for the amount of calories we were using. Our situation was made all the worse as the instructors sitting on the head table, gorged themselves with second helpings and as much bread as they wanted, washing it down with either beer or red wine. This spectacle only added to our torment, as we used our bread to mop up every last drop of juice, making sure that not a single calorie was left on the plate.

Later on that night, Dias showed us how our lockers were to look each evening. *Appel*, or role call is held twice a day, once in the evening at 10 o'clock and then again at 6 o'clock in the morning. Evening *appel* is also accompanied by a room and locker inspection where every locker must be identical. Our clothes must also be cleaned and folded to a width of exactly 30cm, and in addition to this, six of us would also be on guard every night. So that given we were only eleven in number, we could look forward to 'stagging on' every other night.

Although we had initially moaned at the state of this place, it became apparent whilst preparing for *appel* that there was a certain advantage to living in such a shithole. Because it didn't matter how much we swept our room out, it stilled looked a mess, giving those of us who were not on guard more time to prepare our lockers.

Dave, in his own unique style summed it up as he was sweeping: 'It's like me Mam always says. No matter how much you try, you can't make chicken soup out of chicken shit'

Bill looked up at me giggling.... 'Hey.... I bet his Mam doesn't take grief off anyone'

It was Sergeant Heimer who took *appel* for those of us who were not on guard and it was a surprisingly chilled out affair. A few pairs of boots went flying across the room because the soles had not been polished, but apart from that and a word of caution not to let it happen again, there was no real fuss made. I was thinking that maybe he was going easy on us and leading us into a false sense of security because it was our first *appel*. But as I dove into my sleeping bag to maximise the next few hours of precious sleep, I felt so knackered I was just relieved to have made it through the first day. One day over....Twenty-seven more to go!

After what seemed like only five minutes of sleep, we were awakened by our alarm clock in the form of Dais's screaming voice followed by his boot at the bottom of the bed. Our breakfast consisted of a baguette of bread shared between three, a motorway café size plastic pot of jam each, and to wash it down there was hot sweet black coffee. If you didn't previously take sugar in your coffee, you did now, as this was the only hot drink of the day and made a welcome change to cold water.

Before daylight, we had cleaned our rooms, the washroom, and swept the outside area like a police forensic team for anything that wasn't a part of the natural landscape....and a few things that were. Dias followed our police line and anything we missed would be instantly punished with twenty press-ups by the whole group, which led to a few disgruntled noises directed at Pal who was deemed to be walking around with his eyes closed.

The morning PT that followed was a one-hour run led by Pinto. This was our first real run in five weeks and within a mile or so I could feel the cold damp air that I was gulping down in huge quantities, begin to burn the back of my throat and make me retch. With my heart feeling like it was about to burst through my chest, try as I might I started to drop off the pace as Pinto glided effortlessly along the deserted country paths, up the steep valley slopes and through the thick forests. There was never a break in his pace and not once did I see him look back to check on our progress. Paul, Andre and Didier were right on the Adjutant's shoulder, with myself in fourth place about forty yards back and the rest of us strung out until Bill and Pal could be seen trailing in the distance.

By the time we'd reached the farm my lungs were still burning and my legs felt like jelly. But instead of being able to recover we were immediately forced to do press ups until Pal and Bill finally arrived, where they were greeted with a torrent of abuse from Pinto. Pal was fast beginning to stand out, and didn't seem to be doing anything to adhere himself to the rest of us either. It was pretty obvious that we were going to be fucked around by the instructors, even if we performed well, that's the nature of basic training. But there was no need to ask for second helpings, and so far we seemed to be spending most of our time in the press-up position thanks to Pal. If you weren't prepared to give 100% effort all the time, then you might as well paint a large target on your chest.

By far the most enjoyable lesson of the day though was our weapons training. Dias brought out the FAMAS, which is the standard issue assault rifle for all Legionnaires. This was to be our bread and butter and we would have to learn how every single component worked and be able to strip it down and put it back together again blindfold. The FAMAS was a fantastically versatile and very light weapon. It could fire single shot, fully automatic or three-round bursts, and could also launch grenades, either by holding it like a rifle or placing the butt onto the ground and using a separate sighting system to fire it like a mortar. Another feature was that the magazine was situated behind the pistol grip which reduced its overall length. But unlike the British SA80 that was of a similar design, but suffered from only being able to be fired right handed, the FAMAS within a few seconds could be made to fire from either the left or right shoulder.

Dias taught us the five main parts of the rifle and any mistakes we made when asked a short while later to repeat them, meant a sprint to the bottom of the valley and back. Due to the language barrier, all of the foreigners ended up with at least a couple of trips down the hill, but the sting in the tail for our French-speaking *bi-nomes* was that they would have to accompany us, as it was deemed a failure on their part as well. Didier was not impressed at having to run for my failings, but at least being pissed off wiped the smugness off his face, and I was toying with the idea of making another mistake just to wind him up some more. But my boots were starting to rub and so I thought better of it. Although being the right size, they were too narrow and I had already asked Dias back in Aubagne if there was a possibility of changing them for a bigger pair. He had just looked at me for a second, before asking if I was fucking mad and then without waiting for an answer had walked off.

After a pathetically inadequate lunch of beans and bread, we spent the afternoon practising marching and learning a song that would become our anthem, *Soldat De La.*

I found the singing practice a welcome rest to the normal routine of sprinting everywhere as if your hair was on fire, because all it consisted of was slowly marching around the fields at a snail's pace over and over again. It was also taught standing still or marching on the spot, but either way we were not using up too much of our precious energy, because I had only been here just over twenty-four hours and it already felt like my throat had been cut. I felt that we were being trained like athletes, but on a starvation diet and to make our situation even worse, it was freezing cold, which meant we were shivering most of the time using up even more calories.

The reason though for our 'relaxed' afternoon was that we would be night marching about 15km in full kit, which consisted of rifle, spare boots, complete change of clothes, sleeping bag and steel helmet. Sergeant Heimer would be leading our group and he explained that anyone who fell behind would be charged with deserting in possession of a rifle, which was a 30 days in jail offence after which you would re-start the farm. Oh, and as an added incentive your *bi-nome* would also receive the same sentence for failing to stop you. As I was used to walking a fair amount in North Wales, the 15km was not particularly worrying me, but my feet were, and I was thinking about stuffing sport socks down the insides of my boots to protect my ankles that were already being rubbed raw, when Didier came over, and with that bloody superior look that was permanently etched into his face told me that jail was not in his plan and so not to mess up. I was purposely non-committal in reply and informed him that I didn't care about a month in jail, or 'his plan' for that matter either, which sent him back to the other French speakers moaning about me. The truth was, that doing time didn't feature high on my 'to do list' either, but the thing about this place was that I was finding it incredibly frustrating not being able to understand the orders and I didn't need some patronising twat looking down his nose at me and huffing every time I asked for a translation.

The weather was with us on the march and although being cold, there was no wind and not a cloud in sight, which meant that whatever happened at least we would be dry. Heimer set a steady pace that never altered whether we were going up or down hill, and the peacefulness of the night was only broken by the odd cough or a piece of kit being made more comfortable. The constant pace slowly sapped my strength and I began to find it mentally more challenging than I'd first imagined. Not being told how far we'd been marching, or that the next checkpoint was only a short distance away etc, was not something most of us had dealt with before, and it was more difficult than you might think. It was impossible to pace myself, which is something that most people do whatever their level of fitness, whether it's, 'I'll just give it five more minutes on the rowing machine,' or 'I'll just run to the next lamp post.' Because pacing yourself in this way is a great way of motivating yourself. Here though it was much tougher, because 'March at my pace until I tell you to stop,' requires a completely different attitude. You had to push hard all the time and just hope you'd be stopping in the next few minutes....not the next few hours.

With my toes and heels starting to sting I could feel blisters starting to form which more than just hurting, were really annoying me. I'd never suffered from blisters before and feeling a bit sorry for myself, it just felt like more bollocks to deal with on top of everything else. I'd considered myself reasonably fit, but I was under no illusion that I was some kind of superman. I knew that I was going to have to give everything to get through the next four weeks, without the hindrance of my feet being in shit state. But with the 'Farm' appearing in the distance, I hoped that my boots would become more comfortable with time.

The Farm

After a week at the farm I was physically knackered and for everyone life had begun to evolve around the same two precious commodities. Food and Sleep had become the most important things in the world and it seemed that we were getting less and less of both. Everything we did was thought of in these two terms. French lessons for example were enjoyable, not because we were learning French, but because we were sitting down. It even felt like we were getting slower on our morning runs not quicker, which seemed to be the exact opposite of what basic training was all about. Presumably our fitness should be improving, not deteriorating.

A couple of the lads had even started scavenging from the bins, and I suppose it was only a misplaced sense of personal dignity and self respect that stopped the rest of us. But no matter how hungry I get, I hope I don't ever start fighting over bits of discarded bread!

We also smoked the last of our cigarettes during the week and for the smokers amongst us, the last couple of days have been hell. But to our eternal gratitude our agony was eased this morning when we were issued tobacco. And in a show of unity, even the non-smokers took their rations and handed them out.

Despite these hardships though I can sense a good spirit in the camp and mentally I feel strong. We are starting to think as a group and are learning that although Dias is a tough task master and will come down hard on anyone who is not putting the effort in, he is fair. If you follow his rules, do not deviate and always give 100%, then he will leave you alone.

My feet are not faring quite so well, and after a second twenty-kilometre march a few days after the first, my feet are beginning to worry me. I just cannot get enough time in between the marches to allow them to heal and it's frustrating the hell out of me. I know

I'm capable of walking the distance, but towards the end of the second march, every step I took was like walking on hot coals. With the situation only set to get worse as the distances increase over the next weeks, I had reluctantly asked to see Pinto, who after throwing a paddy because I was not prepared to put up with the pain, threw a mess tin at me and told me to 'Fuck off.'

Another problem we have to deal with is that we have not been given any time to wash our clothes. But they are always expected to be clean and by the end of the first week, everyone has run out of fresh socks. I know that for me it's not just a case of walking around with smelly feet. I cannot afford not to keep my open sores clean, so I take a chance and at night during one of my guard shifts, sneak into the wash rooms with a bar of soap and give my feet a good scrub. It's agony pulling away bits of dead skin, but the alternative is to let the sores turn septic, so it's worth taking the risk of being caught. And unless Dias makes an unexpected check-up I should be alright, but I don't want to think about the consequences if I'm found. Fortunately I'm OK and even have enough time to wash a pair of socks.

And so with our morale lifted from our new rations of tobacco, we spent the day chopping wood and piling it onto the back of the truck under the watchful eye of Dias, who ensured that we didn't chat or wander off, which made the place feel more like a prison camp than basic training. But at least it was pleasant enough work and we were pretty much left alone. We were then marched back up the valley to the 'Farm' practising our singing and with another day almost ticked off, were even beginning to enjoy ourselves, until we were met by Pinto who was waiting for us by the gate.

His news hit us like a sledgehammer blow out of nowhere and as well as being completely devastated I was amazed how open and frank he was. He was no longer excited and animated, but calm as he explained that it had been decided, against his will, that our numbers were too few to continue and so we will be leaving in the morning to join another company that had just started their 'Farm'. And unfortunately there was no alternative but for us to start the 'Farm' from scratch.

He explained how proud he'd been to have known us, even for just a week. And that he was sorry he couldn't continue our training. That our new company had a 'different approach to training,' where there was less emphasis on teaching the skills of soldiering and more on discipline. But he told us to remember that they didn't represent all Legionnaires and that we had already shown ourselves to be strong.

He explained that we needed to show that strength and adapt quickly to change. And with a final salute he dismissed us with the words:

'Jusqu'au bout, à tout prix'

I found Bill sitting on the edge of his bed with his head in his hands staring at the floor. 'I can't start this shit again mate. Not for a third time.'

He looked dejected and I didn't really know what to say. Somehow 'chin up mate' seemed a bit hollow, but I remembered his 'medic' stories from Aubagne and so asked if he would look at my feet.

His diagnosis was not great. 'Just try and keep them clean because they won't heal over. Not with the shit food and marches we're doing. I'll see what I can rob from the first aid kit when Dias is not looking.'

I pulled my boots back on and started to pack my gear, trying not to think about the 'different approach to training' that Pinto had spoken of. If the truth be known I didn't want to know and so refrained from asking Bill, who normally had a pretty good idea of these things. But having seen how he was, I knew it wouldn't be pleasant.

As the truck pulled out of the 'Farm' I looked back with a certain sense of regret. We had only been there a week, but it had felt like three and maybe it was a case of 'better the devil you know,' but I had grown almost fond of the place. Things there had become familiar and it was this familiarity that gave it a sense of security. The fact we had been told our new 'Farm' was more modern, hadn't really changed our minds, and it was ironic to think none of us were looking forward to leaving.

We did have one advantage though. We had a weeks' worth of experience over the other recruits, which might not seem a lot, but in this place it almost made you a veteran. As we sat on the truck I noticed that we already looked different, we were losing weight and the crispness of our uniforms had disappeared. Our berets were shaped properly and I was thinking that we looked more like soldiers and less like civilians wearing military uniforms. With these mixed feelings of apprehension and confidence, it wasn't long before I was concentrating on that other precious commodity that was always in short supply...sleep, and closed my eyes.

REVE....Dais's piercing voice which had acted as our never failing alarm call over the last week sparked us back into life, and a cigarette and gulp of water made me feel human again.

The tailgate on the truck crashed open and the shouting started immediately.

Grabbing armfuls of kit we sprinted up the concrete stairs and dumped our gear in our new billet, which was still only half finished having bare brick walls and exposed wires. Throwing our stuff onto the nearest spare beds we ran back outside where Didier received a kick from one of our new instructors, before we lined up in three ranks alongside the other recruits. The guy next to me had a swollen lip and our numbers had now increased to about twenty five. Dias and Sergeant Himer were to stay and our new platoon commander was a young French Lieutenant, who after a short introduction passed over to the Sergeant Chef. This is a senior Sergeant rank and he would be known to us as simply 'the Chef.'

The Chef was a big intimidating looking guy who possessed that psychotic stare that turns all but other psychopaths to stone. And you didn't need to be a psychologist to figure him out. He was a bully, and by the look of things the worst type of bully, because he was obviously the guy in charge....whatever the Lieutenant might think. He explained that here, he made the rules and whatever he decided....went! There was no one to oversee him, no one for us to complain to and nowhere to escape to if we wanted to desert. But he invited us to try all the same, as hunting us down was one of his favourite pastimes.

I was starting to think that the previous week had been like a holiday camp by comparison and I glanced over at the other instructors. Dias was wearing his usual emotionless expression, but the weedy-looking fucker with rat features who had kicked Didier seemed to be lapping it up.

'Rat boy' was what was known as a 'fut fut', which is a rank given to those Legionnaires held back after basic training to help with the next intake of recruits. Consequently they had never served in a combat regiment and with only a very few exceptions were universally loathed. It took a special kind of scum bag to volunteer to become a 'fut fut' instead of going to a regiment. But the carrot for them was that within twelve months they were placed on the Corporals' course.

It is certainly true that every bully has a detestable spineless sidekick. And Rat boy was obviously the Chef's.

The food here was even more depressing than before, as now the same size piece of bread was split between four of us instead of three, and so I imagined that even the bins in this place took reservations.

Based on our previous week's experiences I was sort of looking forward to the French Lesson that was planned after dinner as this usually consisted of being seated, and besides, it was pissing it down outside. But unfortunately I hadn't yet appreciated the sadistically creative mind of the Chef who issued us with spades as we formed up in just our combat fatigues.

Within minutes the icy Pyrenean rain had penetrated our cotton jackets, and our bare shaved heads only added to the discomfort as we waited in silence for the Chef to appear and issue his orders. After half an hour I was freezing and was tensing my muscles to stop myself from shivering when the Chef appeared from an upstairs window holding an empty beer bottle. It was thrown in our direction and a few of us scattered to avoid being hit, which seemed to enrage the Chef even more. Hurling abuse at us about being cowards or something, we were ordered not to move as he lined up for a second throw. It was like a drunken game of human tenpin bowling and he launched another empty. This time no one moved and fortunately it glanced off someone's shoulder before smashing on the floor.

But he became bored with this entertainment and we were ordered to repeat a phrase in French which roughly translated as, 'I'm digging a hole with a spade', before being ordered into the field to start digging in pairs whilst shouting the phrase out loud.

I found Didier in the dark and we started removing the sods of grass and placing them neatly to one side.

'The Chef ....he is fucking cunt'

I'd not heard Didier swear before and it made me smile. It made him seem more human and less pompous somehow and we decided on a plan that it would be better for one of us to dig, whilst the other rested and shouted the phrase out now and again. The trouble was that digging was the only way to keep even slightly warm, but at least the rain would hopefully keep the Chef inside. We continued digging like this for an hour or so, swapping over every ten minutes until it was past midnight when we noticed the Chef marching towards our trench. Didier jumped to his feet and starting digging furiously, but it was too late and the Chef's boot caught him in the chest throwing him back into the mud. I stopped digging and looked up, which was a mistake and he grabbed me by the collar, almost lifting me off the ground.

'Problem....you English shit?'

'No Chef!'

'Then dig....and don't let me catch you sitting around again.'

He moved onto the next hole shouting more abuse at its occupiers, and in silence Didier and I started digging again.

I was absolutely furious with hatred for the Chef. Seeing Didier on the receiving end and having to stand there helpless is the most frustrating feeling I have ever felt. How can the Legion put some pissed up bully in charge of our basic training? What could we possibly learn from this prick? He seemed to have carte blanche to rule over us as he saw fit, with no checks or balances to ensure that we were being trained properly. Or maybe the Legion was happy with this method of training? But surely if they wanted to be a modern professional army this was not the way to achieve it!

But with the rain starting to lift a little we took our frustration out on the soil.

As the dawn broke I could see the rest of the platoon spread out over the hillside, methodically digging and shouting out 'the phrase' that we had been repeating over and over all night long. And after having repeated it a couple of thousand times it had become permanently etched onto our minds.

The rain had turned our trenches into a quagmire so that we were standing in six inches of freezing water. Taking a breather was out of the question because our sodden, mud-caked clothes meant that if we stopped digging we would be shivering uncontrollably within a few minutes. We had long since finished our water bottle of cold water, and chain smoking wasn't having any effect on staving off the hunger pains when Rat boy came out and ordered us to fill in our trenches. But this time to the tune of, 'I fill in this hole with this spade'.

Inspired I thought….I wonder which fucking genius thought that one up.

Formed up on the parade ground a miserable hour later, we looked a mess. It was hard to see the green of our uniforms and the ground was littered with bits of mud that was dropping from us. Rat boy brought us to attention for an inspection by the Chef, who was not unsurprisingly disgusted with our appearance and ordered a hosing down to clean us up….which Rat boy would be dishing out.

Huddled together in small groups, the coldness and power of the fire hose nearly knocked us off our feet and left us fighting for breath, as Rat boy made sure every last piece of mud was gone….sadistically prolonging our agony, whilst at the same time poking fun at our situation.

The outside temperature could not have been more than five or six degrees and standing to attention, waiting for the other groups to finish, the pain of the coldness was almost as much as I could bear. I just wanted to move to get some blood flowing when I heard a welcome voice behind me.

'I'm going ram that fuckin' hose down his bastard throat'

It was Dave, who always seemed to have that ability to say just the right thing at just the right time to raise your spirits, and what's more he was right....Fuck them!!!

The day continued as usual; so that an hour later we'd stuffed some bread and coffee down and were running through the forests and hillsides of our surroundings panting like old dogs trying to keep up with the Lieutenant, who after a good night's sleep and hearty breakfast was lambasting us for slowing down. And by the time we'd stumbled our way back to the farm, it seemed to take forever before the tailenders eventually turned up; all of whom were immediately met with a punch from the Chef who had turned up to add his two pence worth.

The morning and afternoon were then spent combat training, which actually just consisted of running up and down hills in full kit and copying down a few notes that most of us didn't understand. But by the time we'd had our dinner and were getting ready for our evening class, someone noticed that we were one short.

Again we were counted and again we were a man down! In the confusion and tiredness of the day, it seemed that Schuhmann, an eighteen-year-old German lad, had managed to slip away unnoticed.

The Chef, having been informed came storming into the classroom and after hurling chairs around the place, drew his pistol and slammed it down on the table.

You could have heard a pin drop as the entire class froze like rabbits caught in the headlights, and we waited for what seemed like forever for the Chef to make his next move.

He seemed to be holding everyone's stare simultaneously as his fingers slowly gripped around the pistol and I was trying to convince myself that this was some kind of act for our benefit. But I could see that it wasn't as the Chef looked from person to person as if he was choosing his victim.

The tension was incredible and I could see Pal at the front of the class bending his knees, trying to reduce his six and a half foot frame to blend in with everyone else, when Dias burst in.

'Chef....the lieutenant wants to see you'

Never had any of us been so glad to see Dias, but whose entrance I thought was a bit too well timed to have been a coincidence. He never spoke much, but you knew that nothing much got by Dias and he was altogether a different type of Legionnaire than the other instructors. Together with Heimer, you could tell that this wasn't their way. They were passionate when they spoke of their Regiment, were enthusiastic when teaching us, and recently lessons with them had become something to look forward to.

Mobilised into small search parties, each led by an instructor we set off into the countryside to track down poor Schuhmann, who by this time had a couple of hours' head start on us, and deep down I was hoping it was going to be enough time for him to get clear away.

Most of us had more sympathy with Schuhmann than the instructors and this showed, as we carelessly hacked our way through the undergrowth, torn between not wanting to find him on one hand and wanting to get back to the farm to sleep on the other.

It was a cloudless full moon night and the Pyrenees could clearly be seen climbing up in front if us, and in the stillness of the evening they stood out like a giant barrier caging us in. On the other side was Spain and for anyone thinking of deserting, Spain spelt 'freedom'. Dressed only in a green tracksuit with no money or identity papers, it was going to be difficult, but if Schuhmann ran hard and kept off the main roads it might just be possible to get far enough away. Once over the border and into Spain, he could then make his way to the German Embassy.

It was a big task for anyone and unfortunately a few hours later, we heard that it had been too big. Stupidly walking down the road he had been caught by the Chef and our search was called off.

It was the early hours by the time we had trudged back up the valley side and reached the farm which was already a hive of activity. Depressingly I could see the other recruits filing outside laden with beds, lockers and all kinds of other personal kit. Stumbling down the stairs I spotted Bill carrying a rucksack under each arm.

'What the fuck's going on now?'

'The Chef's decided we're going to have a room inspection outside....We've got 30 minutes to get it sorted'

'Where's Schuhmann?'

Bill nodded his head in the direction of the flag pole, dumped his stuff and ran back inside.

Slumped at the bottom of the flag pole, with his head hanging forward, Schuhmann was motionless. His wrists had been bound together behind the flag pole, as had his ankles, so that it was impossible to stand up, and he was forced into a sort of kneeling position. I could see blood on his face and the sight frightened me, but as I turned away I was caught by a slap in the face.

It was Rat boy who had seen me staring.

'Get your fuckin' kit downstairs now.....unless you want to join him?'

After half an hour of our frantic effort to recreate our billet outside, the Chef took less than a minute to find fault and ordered a re-inspection in an hour's time. We had already learnt that this was more or less standard procedure with inspections, which always failed first time around. And then it was a just question of how sadistic the reviewer was as to how many times they kept on failing us. The principle was simply to fuck us about until they got bored. The trick for us, was to look busy by making the odd improvement here and there, whilst making the best use of the time, which in my case meant sorting out the sores on my feet which hadn't been tended to in a couple of days.

At gone four in the morning we were let back inside to catch an hours' sleep after putting our room back together. But poor Schuhmann was left outside.

The morning brought no mention of the night before as we formed up for our daily run next to Schuhmann, as if he was not even there. The talk the night before had been pretty much entirely about what would happen to him. Some thought he would carry on with us and others made wild predictions about spending the next five years in jail if he refused to soldier. Bill though was more pragmatic with a simple:

'Whatever the Chef wants to happen…will happen'

It was with this thought that I felt utterly helpless as later that morning we stood in silence in front of Schuhmann, an unwilling audience to the Chef's twisted version of Legion discipline which was based on fear of your superiors. And he was soon demonstrating the power that came with his position, randomly grabbing individuals by the collar and asking them if they too were wanting to desert. He paced up and down shouting out words like Honour, Courage and Camaraderie as if they somehow justified the treatment of Schuhmann. On and on he ranted before stopping by the flag pole and kicking Schuhmann in the bollocks which forced him to try and curl up to protect himself. This had been made impossible though due to his ankles and wrists being tied behind the pole, which left him incapable of turning away and completely exposed the front of his body.

One side of his face was already swollen from a punch the night before and it was heartbreaking to watch him making futile attempts to dodge the fists, feet and knees of the Chef - which came raining down until he had satisfied his anger.

We'd been told to watch, but I looked down at my feet unable to make any sense of what was happening in front of us. Never had I imagined that we would be forced to watch such violence meted out by such a psychopath. Where was the Lieutenant? He was the senior rank here and his absence spoke volumes. Or maybe I was fooling myself! Maybe the Lieutenant was happy for this type of brutality so long as he didn't see it.

For me though, it was impossible to watch and the feelings of sheer helplessness and frustration mixed with the anger at the unjustness of it all meant that it would have been easier to take the beating than to be a spectator. Seeing a fellow recruit suffer in such a way created a hatred for the Chef that I had never felt for anyone.

Having made his point, he turned and headed back towards the farm, leaving Rat boy to cut down Schuhmann who slumped to the ground coughing up blood, where he was left until the Military Police arrived to take him back to Castelnaudary.

We were given the afternoon to prepare our kit for a night march, which was Legion code to pack your rucksack as quickly as possible and then take the time to get your personal admin sorted out before grabbing a few hours' sleep. We had not really slept for the last couple of nights and we were dead on our feet, but the morning's events had shocked most of us and we found ourselves sitting around in groups mulling over what might happen next.

For the first time since being at the farm, Dave, Bill, Paul and I were chatting in English, which we all knew was an absolute forbidden. I don't think that we didn't care about the rules, but just felt compelled to be around other people that you could converse with in your own language. It was somehow consoling and allowed us to draw strength from the group. Dias though was on the prowl and our heads sunk as he came around the corner whilst we were in mid conversation.

'Alright?'

'Er yes Corporal'

'Is your kit ready for the march?'

'Yes Corporal'

'Good'

With that he continued on his way, leaving us all a little dumbfounded as to why we weren't either in the press-up position or rubbing our sternums for having been caught speaking English.

Being spoken to in such a familiar way by an instructor was unheard of in the Legion. They never praised you when you performed well and never showed any signs of anything but utter contempt for us, so to be almost friendly had left us speechless.

I think that even Dias had been disgusted by the Chef's brutality and I like to think that maybe he wanted us to know that not everyone in the Legion would act in the same way. He could not stand up to the Chef, but that didn't mean he agreed with him.

After managing to sleep for a while, I was sorting out my feet in preparation for the march when Buchy ran past calling for Andre.

Apparently no one had seen him for a while and he was nowhere to be found!

Surely not Andre as well!

I quickly sorted out the laces on my boots and pulled the rest of my kit together as fast as I could, instinctively knowing that within seconds we would be formed up outside being interrogated.

The Chef's fury was monumental. Completely enraged that after his treatment of Schuhmann that someone could show such defiance as to desert again, he was almost lost for words. Accusing us of cowardice for not stopping a fellow recruit from going AWOL, he vowed that we would all suffer for our part in this conspiracy. No one would be able to get away with defying the Legion in the way we had.

Left to mull things over on our own, it was obvious that no one knew anything and no one would have said anything anyway. I liked Andre and over the last few weeks we had become mates. If he had asked me for help in leaving, I would have gladly given it. But as it was he had made the decision on his own, knowing what the consequences would be if he was caught. The thought of this I was sure would provide him with all the motivation he needed and being a strong runner, I hoped that he was running for his life and keeping off the roads. With a little bit of luck along the way, hopefully he could make it over the border and would be sipping beers on the Costa before the end of the week.

For the rest of us though, thoughts of sitting on the beach were a long way off and we were all expecting another search party, but instead only the Chef would search for Andre in the jeep and we would continue with the planned march. At least this would mean no more Chef for the next few hours.

Heimer, as usual set a steady pace that never faulted but I could think of nothing else except how Andre might be getting on as we hiked in silence through small farmsteads and across hills. I was hoping that he would not be there when we returned and the thought of having to watch Andre suffer the same fate as Schuhmann was unthinkable. Watching a mate going through that would be too much! With a good lead though and only the Chef after him, his biggest worry would be being grassed up by the locals or spotted by the civilian police. A skin head and a green army tracksuit were not exactly inconspicuous, but I just hoped that he would make it.

My other thought during the march was about the sores on my feet that had opened up after the first ten kilometres, making the last ten agony, as each step rubbed a little more at my toes and heals until it was difficult to focus on anything other than the pain. I tried to ignore it by thinking of home and what I would do on my first leave, which helped a little. My spirits were lifted even further when I saw that the jeep had still not returned as we marched back through the farm gates in the early hours, marching in step and singing the company song.

A few days later there was still no sign of Andre, which hopefully meant he was safely away, and life at the farm had hit a depressing low. Morale was non-existent and we had started to fight amongst ourselves over the most irrelevant of things, which the instructors never did anything to stop, making us feel like a pack of wild dogs caged by their masters, subservient to their every whim, and longing for freedom.

This is certainly not how I envisaged soldiering to be. Sure I knew things would be tough, but I could not honestly say that so far I'd learnt much about the skills of soldiering, such as map reading, camouflage and concealment, tactics etc. I knew what it was like to starve. I knew what it was like to go for days with little sleep. I had learnt that even the basic things took longer than normal when tired and hungry. I had felt anger, frustration and disgust at watching a fellow recruit being beaten by a drunken bully. I had learnt that my body was capable of a lot more than I had previously given it credit for. I had learnt that if you got angry and pissed off enough, it could distract you from pain. I had learnt that it was only silly pride that stopped you from dusting off a perfectly edible piece of bread from the bin. And I had also learnt that whatever background or culture you came from, once you peeled away a few surface layers, it's pretty much the same things that make us all tick.

These were the things that the Legion was teaching. But the final exam was still a few weeks away and it seemed that the instructors were delighting in our suffering. After a couple of weeks at the farm, I could not say that things were becoming easier, it was just that the bullshit wasn't such a surprise anymore!

One thing that was noticeably improving though was our singing which we practised for hours most nights, marching on the spot and stopping only to do fifty press-ups or to sprint across the field and back if our tone was not what was required. It did give us a sense of achievement though, which in this place was a rare commodity. We could hear our own progress and each night we sounded a little more like the Legionnaires I'd seen back at Castel.

Kepi Blanc

Since Andre's desertion, we had seen less of the Chef and I think the Lieutenant had to finally step in and taken control. I guess having to explain one desertion to his superiors was bad enough, but two would have been classed as sheer incompetence.

This is not to say that suddenly things all became touchy feely though. The Chef was still in charge, but he just became a little more subtle in his methods and as an unarmed combat instructor, he had the perfect excuse. Later that week he took us for two and three-hour long sessions. These lessons had more to do with aggression and toughening us up, rather than providing us with any tactical advantage on the battlefield. If we could no longer use our rifles and had to get into a punch-up with the enemy, then I guess things would not exactly be going to plan. But that said, maybe the world would be a better place if armies could settle their differences by way of a huge punch-up rather than the mass devastation of modern warfare. The Chef though, just saw it as a great opportunity to beat us up under the pretence of teaching us something about self defence. The lessons themselves were absolutely knackering, starting with a half-hour run though the forests in boots and full kit, before we found a suitable clearing well away from the farm to start the session. But not before another half an hour of push-ups, sit-ups, forward rolls, backward rolls, climbing trees, fireman lifts and anything else he could think of to sap our energy.

During our first lesson, the Chef stood at the front and called Pal out to demonstrate a particular technique, asking him to try and punch him in the face (an offer most of us would have jumped at). The punch was blocked and followed by an elbow to the throat and a Judo throw. And once on the floor he was then held in a wrist lock which left him coughing violently, fighting for his breath and frantically tapping the floor with his free hand to show he'd had enough (not that he had any influence on when the Chef let go). This technique he demonstrated three or four times before Pal had served his usefulness and another unwilling victim in the form of Bill was called out to act as his second punchbag of the session. Much as I tried to take this as seriously as the Chef, there was a slightly comical element to the whole affair as the Chef would create different scenarios (most of them completely unrealistic) where he thought his Jackie Chan karate chops would prove invaluable. But to me it all just seemed a bit 'Walter Mitty.' I couldn't help but snigger under my breath when the Chef pretended to be leaning against an imaginary bar sipping on his imaginary Pastis, as Bill tried to tiptoe up behind him and grab him by the throat, where at the last second the Chef would spin around (a move which wouldn't have looked out of place on the dance floor) and deck him; claiming he had seen him in a strategically placed imaginary mirror. The whole thing was hilarious and I could see Dave staring at the floor trying his best not to laugh out loud as the Chef ordered us into pairs to practise a few throws, insisting we did not take it easy on each other.

Maybe it would have been easier just to drink in places where people didn't try and tiptoe up on you from behind!!

He had not intended it, but the Chef had given me the first laugh since I'd been at the 'Farm.' And as we ran back, I remembered how long it had been since I'd laughed properly and more importantly, how good it felt. Maybe the fact that we could now find humour in these situations, where we once would have felt nothing but dread, meant that we were finally beginning to improve.

After getting through the next couple of days our morale started to improve, as psychologically we started to gain the upper hand when it struck us that 90% of the 'farm' was in your head. As we pushed into the middle of week three, we could finally begin to see the light at the end of the tunnel (the first of many tunnels admittedly, but light all the same). In less than a week we would begin the 'Kepi Blanc' march which meant that we could now count on one hand the number of days left in this place. The fact that the hardest march of our lives faced us at the end of the 'farm,' was seen by most of us as welcome news. It would hopefully mean a reduction to the bullshit and bullying, and the thought of this lifted our spirits enormously. They only had a few days left to try and break us, but after three and a half weeks in this place….they had no chance.

I started splitting the days in half which made them more manageable to cope with, until the 'Kepi Blanc' march was only a day away. Rat boy had been overdosing on bullying tablets as he grasped to get his final fix of punching and kicking people in a last ditch effort to push us over the edge. But the harder he tried the more pathetic he looked. We had been taught to always look a superior directly in the eye when spoken to and had discovered that even with an expressionless face a stare could say almost anything you wanted it to. From 'however hard you try you cannot break me' to 'if I ever get the opportunity I'm going knock the fuck out of you. You runty little bastard'

It might sound strange to say, but you knew that every word was understood, and it was also becoming evident that Rat boy had lost the one thing he desired the most….our respect.

He was trying everything he could think of to humiliate us and after Buchy had been caught putting a tomato into his pocket whilst cleaning the pots and pans in the kitchens, Rat boy ordered him to eat a whole sack full in front of us and wash them down with a couple of litres of milk. He was then run ragged doing push-ups, sit-ups and short sprints until the inevitable happened and he was sick, which looked quite funny seeing someone spew up what looked like a tomato smoothie. Rat boy thought this was wonderful, but the trouble was that so did Buchy, who was a greedy bastard at the best of times and thought that being sick was a fare pay-off for being able to stuff his face. Pissed off and frustrated with the failure of his plan Rat boy ordered us to sprint across the field and in temper started hurling rocks after us. But after weeks of similar treatment we had learnt to keep one eye looking over our shoulder and dodged them easily. Being the useless fucker that he was, Rat boy had even failed to wear us down.

An hour before the march the farm was a hive of purposeful and controlled activity, as we busied ourselves with checking and re-checking our kit. I'd got up early and spent the time preparing my feet, carefully constructing makeshift pads out of cut up pieces of sports socks, to protect the open sores on my ankles and heels. In the absence of any plasters, it was the best I could do and I was grateful to Bill who had managed to get hold of some surgical tape to hold them in place. It was imperative that I got my feet as comfortable as possible, as there would be no stopping once we'd started. The same went for the rest of our gear and around the room I could see people adjusting straps on their rucksacks, trying them on and then making more little adjustments here and there. Without the modern straps that can be lengthened or shortened whilst being worn, our old-fashioned rucksack had to be just right before setting off. If it was even slightly uncomfortable at the start you could guarantee it would be agony after a couple of hours, so it was worth spending the time now getting it right. This went for every piece of kit that could potentially rub or hinder you in any way, and to do it properly took the knowledge that only comes with experience, which we did not exactly have by the bucket load. But I remembered all the marches we had done over the last month to ensure that I would not be held back by a loose buckle here or a bootlace tied too tight there. And with our preparation over, we formed up outside for the last time.

There was a real buzz of excitement mixed with apprehension, with a sense of just wanting to get going. We had all been through a lot and for me the mental strength needed had much of the time been greater than any physical. We all had to deal with things in our own way and although very much a team that was reliant on each other, there had also been a tremendous amount of personal determination needed. There had been times for all of us, because of the way the Legion works, when our reliance on ourselves and being able to make our own decisions had been thoroughly tested. The Legion did not spoon-feed you in any way. They didn't give you enough sleep, food or set aside any time to wash your clothes and kit; so it was up to you to find time to sleep, find extra food, and to make sure your kit was always clean, even if you were on the go twenty-four hours a day. They really didn't care how you did it....they just expected the required result. For me this was obvious from the way I'd had to sort out my own feet. The instructors didn't care whether my feet were cut to ribbons or not. It was my problem to find some antiseptic and my problem to keep them clean and bandaged. Nor was I any different to many of the other recruits stood alongside me, who had all had their own difficulties to deal with. As a result, as well as bonding as a unit, we were also more self reliant and confident. I would not agree with all of their training methods, but without wanting to sound too clichéd, I did feel different. Not in an arrogant way, just that I knew I could take more. But that said I remember what Bill had said to me about the 'Kepi Blanche' march being the most important thing I would ever do in the Legion. I didn't know whether that was true or not, but I did know that whatever had happened over the last month or so, in one way seemed pretty irrelevant. Because however good or bad we had performed at the farm, it was the next forty-eight hours that would determine whether or not we became Legionnaires. It was now just down to how much we wanted it.

We were driven to a starting point and after a couple of kilometres I was beginning to enjoy the relative tranquillity of the day. We had split into teams and ours, as usual was being led by Sgt Heimer striding out at his normal methodical pace. Having split up from the other two groups, I was actually quite enjoying myself. Bill was in front of me and with no one talking it was the first time that I had appreciated the breathtaking beauty of the surrounding landscape. The scenery was stunning and the snow topped Pyrenees made a majestic backdrop to the lush greenery of the hilly terrain that stretched out in front of us. I wondered if Andre had made it over those mountains in just his tracksuit or whether he had already been caught as some of the others had been speculating, serving out his sentence in jail until the Legion decided what to do with him. I wished him well under my breath. As I looked up, I could hear Bill beginning to pant louder in response to the extra effort needed as we started to climb up a single footpath that snaked its way along the edge of a wooded area on the side of a steep hill. I could feel that my makeshift bandages were still in place, but even so these uphill bits came as a bit of a relief, because although more trying, they placed less pressure on my feet and anything that brought respite to my cuts, however temporary, was more than alright by me. After an hour's hard climb we crested the hill and I stood up straight to fill my lungs with the pure mountain air. The valley which stretched away to our right was dominated by a large fast-flowing river, whose steep impassable stone banks glistened in the light drizzle that had begun to fall. Heimer pointed towards a bridge in the distance, quite some way below us, that looked like the only way to cross the river, and you could just make out seven or eight figures marching in single file towards our side of the valley.

'Lieutenant'

It would have been nice to know whether that meant we were miles ahead or miles behind, but Heimer was not saying and so stopping only long enough for a drink, we continued on our way. As we descended halfway back down the valley side, I could feel my feet begin to sting as my bandages began to move, exposing my sores which opened immediately. I knew from past experience that trying to shift my feet around inside my boots or altering my stride, placing more pressure on the inside of my feet in an attempt to relieve the pain was futile and frustrating, but I tried anyway, cursing my boots every time a rock pressed against the sides causing a sharp burning pain in my heels and toes. I could never have imagined how uncomfortable a pair of boots could be and given that I was not alone in this respect I wondered if this was another trial the Legion was placing in our path. The fact that the boots were uncomfortable was probably a plus to the training staff.

We were heading for a small village at the far end of the valley and we could see clearly the red roof tiles that contrasted the grey stone walls of every building. As we entered past the sign to the village I felt suddenly rejuvenated by the sight of a post office, and by glancing through the window of a small empty bar. This was the closest we had been to civilisation in almost two months and it felt fantastic. There was a barmaid leant against the bar waiting for some passing trade. She looked up and smiled as we passed, to which we all must have collectively stood up straighter and puffed out our chests in response. Sights like these were absolutely price-less and for however short a period lifted our spirits.

I leant my rucksack against the side of a tree and slumped down beside it, relieved to be able to take the pressure off my feet. Even in the cold my back was sodden in sweat and I started to shiver within minutes. We had only half an hour for lunch, but opening our ration packs we'd been supplied with felt like Christmas. This was the first time we'd been given proper rations and tucking into the hot meal cooked up on a little stove felt wonderful. Bill was using the chocolate bar as a sort of spoon to shovel down his meat stew and claimed that nothing had ever tasted better. He asked how my feet were and could only continue to reassure me not to give in....however bad the pain got. Bill though was not looking too good himself and I could see that the morning's march had left him knackered. He was pasty looking and I hoped he would not be the one who dropped out. He had gone through a lot to come back and do all this again and I just hoped that we would both be there tomorrow, standing side by side, placing that Kepi on our heads and singing our hearts out.

Heimer increased the pace in the afternoon and the pain in my feet became excruciating and pretty soon every step felt like I was walking on hot coals. My discomfort was added to by Bill who could not keep up with the guy in front of him and every few minutes he would have to jog to close the gap, as would everyone else behind him. This is how it went on all afternoon and at times the pain became so bad, I just wanted to jack it all in. It was so frustrating to be hindered by something as stupid as ill-fitting boots and to think that I could come all this way and fall at the last hurdle was devas-tating. It was becoming difficult to focus upon anything except my own discomfort, and thoughts of back home were only distracting me for a few seconds before the pain would jolt me back to reality. Grinning and bearing it was not working either, so I tried to think more practically and set myself small goals like 'just make it to the next tree line' etc.

This is how I made it for the last few hours and ones which I can honestly say were the longest in my life, until we rounded a bend in the road and noticed the truck parked up in one of the side fields, signalling the end of the first day.

After setting up our shelters, constructed out of waterproof sheets, I set about taking my boots off and peeling back my socks to inspect my feet. The cuts on my heels and ankles had rubbed bigger and the side of my toe looked like it had been taken to with an electrical sander. My boots had left a perfectly smooth edge, but even more worryingly, the sole of my foot around the heel had started to peel away, leaving a sort of mouth shaped gap, with a flap of skin that was imitating a sort of bottom lip. The whole area had turned white and not being able to place much pressure on it, I called Bill over for a second opinion, who after suggesting trying to 'superglue' it back together, said that all he could do would be to hold it in place with tape and hope it reattached itself once we were back in Castel.

Not that I had any choice, but I taped my feet back together and tried not to walk around too much until morning.

The morning's march was a killer and I don't know how I managed to keep going at times. The pace was quick and my boots felt like they were full of tiny razor blades that caused pinpricks with every step. Bill was not faring much better either and needed constant encouragement to keep closing the gap that kept opening up with the guy in front of him. Heimer was silent throughout and never once shouted at him to keep up and it almost seemed that he was of the opinion that it was up to Bill whether he wanted to keep going or not. It was his job to set the pace and ours to keep up. No allowance or exceptions were made and there were times when I was contemplating stopping. If I'd been given the option I may well have taken it, but I wasn't and just kept focused on achieving the little goals I was setting myself, even if they were getting shorter and shorter. I kept telling myself that if I could just keep going a little longer, the end could not be that far away, but relief came in an unexpected fashion as we started a steep climb an hour or so after lunch. Bill had not spoken much all day and during lunch had slept whilst the rest of us had eaten the last of our rations and drunk as much water as possible. Most of us were too pre-occupied with our own issues to pay him much attention and three-quarters of the way up the hill, he slowed down, stopped and collapsed.

Heimer, who was there almost before he hit the floor, rolled him over, raised his legs with the aid of his rucksack and within a few seconds Bill started to come back around. His complexion was pale grey and his eyes had sunken into his skull, leaving him looking middle-aged even though he was only in his mid-thirties. Heimer ordered him to stay still and told the rest of us to take a fifteen minute break, which came as heaven sent relief for everyone. Most of us were on our last legs anyway for one reason or another and although no one would have wished Bill to collapse, no one was complaining of the break. If we were totally honest with ourselves, he may have been the one who went first, but many of us were not that far behind. Bill collapsing, had inadvertently stopped the rest of us from going the same way and everyone profited as best they could from our unexpected rest.

Whilst Bill was drinking a glucose drip which Heimer had been carrying, and fuelling up on chocolate, I messed around with my laces in a vain attempt to ease the pain before we started back up the hill.

This rest had been a lifesaver for everyone, and even Bill seemed to have perked up now that he was overdosing on glucose and suddenly became chatty, offering me encouragement and even managing to crack a joke about something. He was like a hyperactive child who'd had too many e-numbers and I swear he would have run up the hill if ordered. But as it was, Heimer continued to stomp his way steadily upwards until we reached a plateau. There, not more than a couple of hundred feet away we could see the truck once again and a more beautiful sight I have never seen. A thought crossed my mind that this could be one more sick taunt to knock us down again, so I tried not to get my hopes up and carried on until Heimer turned around.

'C'est fini. Vous êtes tous Les Légionnaires'

And that was it. No big song and dance, just a few words that signalled the end of the march and the reason most of us had put up with the last month. It was hard to believe we'd actually made it.

Here, on the side of some mountain whose name I didn't know, somewhere in the south of France, I had earned the right to wear the famous white Kepi and the rank of Legionnaire. We dumped our kit and I hobbled over to the back of the truck were we were given a bottle of beer and a handful of peanuts. And thirty seconds later I was pissed and enjoying the atmosphere. For the first time in two months we were relaxed and sat around waiting for the other two groups, just enjoying the feeling of being free and the sense of achievement that had come with pushing ourselves further than any of us had even done before. For me it was a real milestone, because I'd only ever just 'done alright' in life, and my school reports had been bang on when they said, 'would do better if he bothered trying.' And it was true, I'd always known I was a bit of a dreamer, but this was different….this was real, and for the first time in my life I felt incredibly proud of myself.

Once we'd all arrived we formed up in three ranks on the side of the mountain. We each had our 'Kepi Blanc' in our hands, waiting in anticipation for the order to put it on for the first time. Bill, Dave, Paul, Didier and Buchy had all made it, even though Buchy had gone the same way as Bill and collapsed. Except instead of being given a drip, Rat Boy had kicked him until he'd started moving again. But none of that mattered now. They'd both made it and I was also glad to see my *bi-nome* Didier, who at times got right under my skin, but was a good bloke deep down and deserved to have passed.

In a simple ceremony we were ordered to place our Kepis on our heads and at that moment we became Legionnaires. We sang *'Soldat De La'*, which made the hairs on the back of my neck stand up and then headed back to Castel in the trucks, where we stopped just outside the main gate and formed up again.

My feet were in bits, but I was determined not to hobble and end up looking like a twat. We marched the Legion's slow march, singing our sombre anthem, through the main gate and past a guard of honour that saluted us as we went past.

It was incredibly moving to be acknowledged and accepted in this way, and although only the first of many hurdles to overcome in the next five years, it was one of the most important.

Chasing Trains

The medic took one look at my feet, told me I was going nowhere and then promptly informed me to have a shower with a bottle of antiseptic he'd given me and report back in a couple of hours.

Of the ten or so of us who were sitting in the waiting room, eight were treated on the spot and two of us were to be seen later. The small hospital at the barracks looked brand new and the shower was my first proper wash in two months. The hot jets of water felt soothing on my muscles and I slumped down in the shower tray and closed my eyes, thinking of nothing for the next ten minutes whilst the steam worked its way under my skin and relaxed my aching frame. My feet stung as I scrubbed the grime out with the antiseptic, but twenty minutes later I felt re-energized and clean. A feeling that felt almost alien.

With my feet clean, the medic went to work and carefully cut away the dead pieces of skin, exposing small craters in my ankles and toes; until he was down to new flesh which meant that he could stop cutting and start packing them out with a sort of thick brown antiseptic gel. The flap on the bottom of my foot had indeed started to reattach itself as Bill had predicted, and the medic told me I would not be leaving for four or five days. And with that he moved on to the other Legionnaire who had been at the 'Farm,' and looking at his foot, started mumbling under his breath.

The Legionnaire's right leg from the knee down was bright red and swollen and I could see a small pussey blister about the size of a penny on the back of his heel. From what I could gather, he had put a piece of tape onto the blister whilst at the farm and then just left it. Now, two or three weeks later it had become infected and was turning gangrenous. The medic must have burrowed an inch or so into his foot, pulling out putrid bits of skin before calling for the doctor, who immediately ordered a drip with penicillin and an ambulance to take him to the military hospital in Toulouse. It was frightening to think that something so serious could develop from a simple blister, so I was glad I'd spent the time washing my feet whenever I'd had the chance. Self inflicted gangrene looked incredibly painful and was definitely not very cool at all.

The crisp clean sheets and comfortable bed gave me eight hours straight sleep and I woke with a sort of hangover, not having had so much sleep in such a long time. I tucked into a breakfast feast fit for kings that consisted of hot chocolate and as much bread, cheese and jam as you could eat. All of which was served around a very civilised large wooden table. It was all I could do to resist the temptation to gulp it down as quickly as possible and I tried to remember where I was. But the biggest advantage about being in hospital was that there was a pay phone in the building.

Although I had to spend most of my time with my feet exposed to the air, so was not allowed off site, I'd managed to get one of the other patients to buy a phone card for me and waited until there was no one around to sneak downstairs. I had been told that the phone was off bounds for me as a new Legionnaire, but the opportunity was too good to miss and I could not resist the temptation of telephoning home.

It was excellent to speak to my mum and dad for the first time in ages and it was brilliant just to catch up and try and briefly explain why I'd joined. They were incredibly understanding under the circumstances, but hearing their voices it felt like I'd been away forever even though I'd left England just ten weeks before. And thinking about it in those terms meant that I still had another four years and ten months to go....Fucking Hell....Put like that it suddenly sounded like an awfully long time!

After a couple of days' rest I was itching to get back into training though. I didn't want to miss out on anything, but a visit from Bill explained that the week was pretty much being given over to cleaning all the kit used at the farm and training would begin again in earnest next week. He did bring me a letter though that had arrived for me and I couldn't believe it when I started reading and saw that it was from Andre. It was fantastic news....he had made it home after a truly epic journey. He had indeed attempted to cross the Pyrenees on foot, travelling only at night, but after a few days had not even reached the lower peaks. Realising the futility of his efforts, he had taken a huge gamble and walked into an Italian Restaurant in one of the villages and explained his plight. Incredibly, they had fed him, given him a change of clothing and had even driven him into Spain, where he had made his way to the Italian Embassy and claimed he was a tourist who had lost his passport. Now back home in Naples, he was planning to go back to Hollywood and plead for his old job back. He wished me well and passed his regards onto the rest of the group. The Legion had obviously not been for Andre and I was genuinely pleased that he had made it home.

With good food and plenty of sleep, my feet healed remarkably quickly and after a week I was back with the group and able to start running again. We now had seven weeks left in Castel and that time would be taken up teaching us the basics of soldiering and learning more about the history of the Legion. At the end of the period there would be a final exam which would determine which Regiment we would be sent to.

There are officially ten Legion Regiments, all with different specialities and dotted throughout the world, from Djibouti in the horn of Africa to the jungles of French Guyana in South America. There was even a small regiment based in Tahiti, although this was unfortunately not available to new Legionnaires. In mainland France there was an Infantry regiment, a Cavalry regiment that used light tanks, an Engineering regiment, and based in Corsica there was the Parachute regiment. You could select your three preferred regiments and would normally be given one of your choices, but if you wanted to join the Parachute regiment, there were normally no more than three or four places available so you had to perform well and get a decent pass mark. Competition was high for the 2eme Regiment Etrangere De Parachutistes (2nd REP) and I had already decided that's where I wanted to go. It had a reputation of being the best. And out of all of our instructors it was

Heimer and Dias, both from the REP that had impressed me the most with their calm, level-headed no nonsense approach. They were the only instructors who actually inspired you in any way and the only ones who actually seemed to know what they were talking about. Apart from being first class bullies, it was difficult to see what other skills the other instructors processed. It was difficult to put into words, but those two just seemed a cut above the others - and besides, as a paratrooper you would earn more money, with the average Legionnaire earning the same as a corporal in another regiment. In terms of money, I had been pleasantly surprised because I'd expected to receive next to nothing. But the Legion was now paid the same rates as the French army which meant that as a 1st Class Paratrooper (more than ten months' service), you would get paid in the region of £1,000 a month. For the moment though most of what little money we did get, seemed to be taken off us to pay into one fund or another, so that after two months, I'd not spent a penny, but still only had a couple of francs to my name.

The pace of life though at Castel never slowed down and far from returning from the 'Farm' as the all-conquering heroes, and putting our feet up, we were still classed as being less than human and about as low on the Legion pecking order as it was possible to be. Rat boy and the Chef were still bullying little shits, the only difference was that they had to be a touch more discreet in their work.

Being back in barracks as Legionnaires also meant we could now be spammed for duties, which included cleaning the canteen, cleaning the sergeants' mess, cleaning the officers' mess or being on guard duty at the main gate for twenty-four hours. Guard was by far the worst and meant not being able to sit down during the day even when not on duty, for fear of creasing your uniform. But whatever the duty, the common theme was usually cleaning some load of old bollocks that belonged to some lazy bastard who couldn't be arsed to clean it for themselves.

On the up side though, our fitness was now much improved and with good food and adequate sleep, our daily runs were noticeably increasing our stamina. Weapons' training with the FAMAS was paramount and we would spend hours on the indoor range, and then even longer cleaning our rifles, which was always done standing up, just to piss us off even more. We were also briefly familiarised with the other weapons that would become the tools of our trade if we ended up in an infantry regiment, which included the 7.62mm machine gun, the 89mm anti tank rocket and the 9mm pistol. But the greatest emphasis was placed on teaching the traditions and the history of the French Foreign Legion, rather than concentrating on the skills of modern soldiering. This seemed strange at first, because I had imagined that after finishing basic training I would be a fairly competent and skilled soldier, but it seemed that was not the purpose of this place. Our regiments would train us in our particular specialities, whilst basic training was all about instilling what it means to be a Legionnaire. And because of this, at times I couldn't wait to get out of there. It wasn't that learning to be a Legionnaire wasn't important to me, but I'd had a stomach-full of cleaning.

The days were long, and at times dragged from six in the morning when they started to ten at night when on a good day they finished. At times, it felt that we were not learning much except how to scrub floors or empty bins, and I lived for the times when we got out of the barracks and into the hills. Marching was still a big part of our training when we did and I had managed to get hold of a decent pair of boots that actually fitted and didn't rub my feet to pieces. These escapes though were few and far between and we were all focused on just making it through these pointless days and getting to our regiments.

This frustration at not doing more soldiering, only added to our sense of worthlessness and it boiled over one day outside the indoor range, when Paul suddenly placed his FAMAS on the floor and refused to move. This notably confused Rat boy whom I don't think had seen anything like it before. Paul who could still not string more than a few words together in French started ranting in broken English, and was going on about being 'crazy' and that 'no fucker' was going to change his mind.'

Rat boy who looked genuinely surprised, shouted and pushed him back in line, but when this didn't work, he didn't know what to do. In his world, he gave an order and it was carried out without question or there would be consequences. But seeing someone just blatantly ignoring him was a first and looking more than a little confused, he ran off and returned a few minutes later with his master. The Chef, only knowing one method of negotiation, punched Paul in the mouth and ordered him back in line. Paul though, in a show of sheer defiance, or maybe madness, got up, repeated his claim that he was crazy (a remark that no one at this stage doubted) and refused to move. It was incredible to see this stand-off, of which there was only ever going to one outcome, as the Chef again punched him in the mouth and leaving him on the floor, turned and disappeared off. I was open mouthed, as Paul had not seemed any more pissed off than the rest of us, so either he had just flipped or this was the best piece of method acting I'd ever seen. But standing there alone, he kept on his rant:

'ME CRAZY

ME LOCO

ME WORK NO MORE HERE'

With the Chef gone we took the opportunity to try and talk to him. But whether he was keeping the act going or not, he was not saying anything and blanked everyone. Whether he'd genuinely flipped or not I couldn't honestly say, but there was no way back now. A simple 'Sorry it won't happen again,' or…'It was just a moment of madness' wasn't going to cut it. Whatever happened was not going to be good and Paul had been here long enough to know it. No one who defied the Chef could expect to get away with it.

The seconds passed slowly as we waited in anticipation of the Chef's return. And he eventually turned up with the PM's who ignored Paul's ranting and slung him into the back of their jeep and headed off in the direction of the guardhouse.

Although I was a bit gob-smacked at the time, I wasn't really surprised by Paul's outburst. Many times I had wanted to punch the walls in frustration or do some damage to something or someone. This place had that effect on people. With its constant insistence on doing things that are completely pointless and the frustration of orders that much of the time seemed designed only to keep our motivation at rock bottom and suppress any sense of at least trying to enjoy our training, or even just making the most of it, there were times when you thought you were about to explode. Just when you think you are starting to understand the rules of the game, they go and change them just to piss you off and to let you know who is in charge. The training seemed designed to instil a sense of worthlessness amongst us and we were all equally despised. No praise was ever heaped on those who were better runners or better shots or who were picking up French quicker. No one was ever given a pat on the back for giving 110%. Here, whether you were the best recruit or worst, it made no difference, we were each a piece of shit. The instructors were from the carrot-and-stick school of training. Except someone had forgotten the carrot, and the situation was made worse by instructors like Rat boy who commanded no authority or respect. It was one thing taking orders from Dias or Heimer, whom you might not like, but at least they knew what they were taking about. They could climb the rope faster than most, run further and quicker, they were crack shots and even if at times they could be cruel and brutal, they were at least respected. Our frustration was at times a constant struggle to control and huge personal effort was required to try and stay level-headed. Whether this meant thinking of home, or counting the days until the end of instruction, it didn't matter as long as you had something to keep your sanity in check. Much of the time it felt like you were in a pressure cooker and with no avenue to vent off steam, it usually boiled over in the form of fighting amongst ourselves. I had forgotten the number of minor punch-ups we had between one another, but normally they were over the most irrelevant of things and they never lasted more than a few seconds at most. I remember having a punch-up with a Rumanian recruit one time over not wanting to pick up a football. One second we were having a friendly kick about and the next we were tearing chunks out of each other. Stupid thing was, we were actually good mates.

Paul's frustration though had unfortunately overflowed at the wrong time and he was now going to pay the price. Hopefully it would work out in the way he wanted, but either way he had gained the respect of the whole platoon; something that was by no means a right of passage in this place and something people like Rat boy would have given their right arm for.

With five weeks left at Castel, time seemed to stand still and whilst in barracks, had become a never-ending cycle of boring mundane routine which comprised in the main of sweeping, mopping and taking orders from some of the most inept, arrogant bastards I have ever met. No doubt they had failed or were unwanted by most units in the Legion and had ended up here and put in charge of the recruits who cleaned the canteen or messes. And their sole purpose was to make our lives as uninteresting and lifeless as possible. I remember a group of us finishing cleaning the Legionnaires' canteen late one evening and grabbing a drink at the coffee machine, and looking out across the running track at a train that was speeding past into the night. No one was speaking as we all watched, and in the silence I was sure that everyone was think-ing the same as me. That they would rather be on that train surrounded by civilians and going anywhere, than stuck in this shit-hole, knee deep in food waste.

Our daily runs though were my only respite from the bore-dom. We ran for miles sometimes along the towpaths of the Canal de Midi with the early morning spring sunshine on our faces. And with a cooling breeze that whistled through the line of trees that separated the canal from the fields, it made for a never failing sense of freedom from the confines of our barracks that were starting to feel more and more like a prison.

Paul was still in jail and making out he was mad in order to be released from his contract. We'd seen him on his daily run in full kit that all prisoners were made to do, with a couple of sacks of sand each in their rucksacks to add to their discomfort. But on seeing us he broke ranks and turning to face us, shouted at the top of his voice

'They can't do this to me man. Don't they know who I am....I'm a fucking movie star!'

We all cheered him back and with that he punched the air, stepped back in line and continued on his way.

It was fantastic to see him in such high spirits and his sense of defiance was more than a little motivating. Maybe they would let him go back to Texas, but for the moment he was not going anywhere except around and around the barracks until he could no longer stand, let alone claim he was a movie star.

A few weeks later Dave was in my room, and announced that he was going to see the Company Adjutant, and tell him he wanted to leave.

'I'm not going make out I'm mad or anything. I'm just going tell him straight that this place is wank and I want out. It's not a patch on the British army and I'm just sick of being treated like a cunt all the time. I want to go back home and just get a normal job. I've done the whole army thing for years and I don't need it again for another five in a wank place like this. I can go back to the British army and get my old rank back if I want. They are desperate to stop the lads leaving....It's just shit here....they haven't got a fucking clue.'

I couldn't help but laugh at the thought of Dave standing in front of the Adjutant, coming to attention, saluting and then saying 'This place is wank and I want out.'

The thing was, that Dave's French was getting pretty good, so gobbing off wasn't going to be an issue, and knowing Dave as I did, he never left people in any doubt as to what he thought. There was never any diplomacy or skirting around the issue with him, it was always straight to the point.

I was disappointed though, as with Andre already gone and Paul unlikely to come back, it would be gutting to see Dave go as well. But he had to decide what was best for him and this is what he had decided on and that was that. I also admired the stand he wanted to take as well, because it would be much easier to ask to be posted to a unit in France, wait for some weekend leave and never come back. With money in his pocket and his ID card, he would be back in Blighty within the day. But Dave said that if was going to leave he would do it properly, and it did cross my mind that it was people with this type of conviction and strength of character that the Legion should be encouraging to stay.

And so with his mind made up he passed in front of the Company Adjutant, who acted as a sort of filter before allowing anyone to see the Company Commander, and five minutes later Dave was back upstairs with a swollen eye and split lip.

'He didn't accept your letter of resignation then mate'

'I don't give a fuck about that cunt.....I've already asked to see him again tomorrow'

On his third attempt and looking like a panda, Dave finally got his chance with the Company Commander who told him there was no way out and if he complained any more, he would make sure Dave got sent to either Djibouti or French Guyana. This meant that he would not be back in mainland France for two years, but not withstanding this threat Dave insisted that he was going nowhere and wanted to leave. And confronted by this type of defiance the Company Commander had no choice but to throw him in jail, where Dave was happy to stay until he was allowed to go home.

After that, things seemed to calm down for a couple of weeks until our last week at Castel when we were busy being put through our final tests. And with Dave and Paul still in jail, any hopes that we had that they would be let out for test week, were quickly destroyed.

I thought it was sad to see them come so far and pack it in so close to the end. But they were men who knew their own minds and had to do what was right for them.

For myself though, although frustrated, pissed off at times and longing to break out of this place, I never seriously thought about leaving. Sure, there were times that I would have rather have been anywhere else, but overall it was still something I wanted to continue with. I had come this far and managing to overcome the physical and mental barriers that had been placed before us had only served to make me more determined to push on and get to my chosen regiment.

In many ways I actually agreed with Dave. This place was rubbish at times and full of the biggest bunch of wankers you would ever want to meet. But it was the French Foreign Legion and maybe it had been my naivety to think that being a Legionnaire was just about jumping out of planes, sprinting around assault courses and doing all of the gung-ho stuff. This place wasn't like that at all; it was all about putting you in the most uncomfortable physical and mental situations and then turning the pressure up and seeing how you coped. Only then….if you could deal with the dull, the boring and the mundane for months on end would you be allowed to progress to the interesting stuff. Putting us all into a glass jar and shaking it about to see what happens might not have been the most sophisticated of training regimens. But they had succeeded in taking a group of civilians from different countries, backgrounds and cultures, who could not even converse with each other, and managed to create a cohesive military unit in a little over twelve weeks.

So with less than a week left, I was determined to do well in the final exams, which were spread over four days and consisted of a timed run around the running track, another in full kit over 5km, as many pull-ups as you could manage, and being able to pull yourself up a 5m cord using only your arms (all those pre-meal aperitifs at the farm had come in useful after all). There was also a test of our knowledge of the traditions of the legion, basic drill, and the most important of all, how good a shot we were!

Everything was scored and an overall pass mark was awarded, either very good, good, average or fail. I achieved a 'good' pass mark and ended up in fourth place overall. Didier was second and Bill was in the bottom half, but considering he had ten years on most of us, he seemed happy just to have passed at all and I actually found myself quite enjoying the final week. Not that I have any great love for exams, but it made a pleasant break from the cleaning, and doing something constructive for once at least gave me a sense of purpose. There was also the prize of being accepted into the Parachute Regiment being dangled in front of me that spurred me on to push myself that little bit further. And I was hoping my efforts had been enough as I waited my turn outside the Captain's office. He would look at where the Legion needed soldiers and would then decide where we would be posted. With only three other people ahead of me in the rankings, I knew I stood a pretty good chance of getting to the 2nd REP, but it would still be down to the wire.

In contrast to the NCOs who always screamed at you, the Officers always spoke in a very clear and purposeful way, checking that every word was understood, and it was in this precise manner, that the Capitaine explained that he only had three places for the REP. And two had already gone.

'Do you deserve the final place?'

I explained something or other about not letting him down and I must have managed to convince him, because he told me I had a place and would be leaving for Corsica in less than a week. It was difficult to describe how good it felt to be told I would be going to the 'Rep,' but anyone who has ever landed the job of their dreams will know exactly what I mean.

Also joining me would be Buchy and Didier, whilst Bill would be heading back to the Legion headquarters and an office job….a decision that he seemed to be more than happy with. And so hanging around outside smoking, the talk was of where and what lay ahead of us. We were all heading off to different parts of the world and it was sad to think that most of us would probably never see each other again. But there was a real sense of excitement of having finally made it through Castel and heading off to our new regiments. But our final treat came a few minutes later and it was one that I would have paid good money not to have missed.

Rat boy and Dias, who had never really hung around together, were walking towards us chatting when Rat boy seemed to throw an insignificant comment back to Dias, who just flipped. And before most of us had had time to blink he'd punched him three or four times in the face, kicked his legs from underneath him and had him pinned to the floor by his throat.

I don't know what it was over, but my first thought was….Great…serves the bastard right.

Since being here, my naive belief in 'what goes around, comes around' had, up to now been by and large disproved. This place was full of people who seemed to get away with the cruellest of behaviour. In fact at times it seemed they were almost encouraged to be cruel. And with people like Rat boy you could see they enjoyed their work. With scum bags like them, it wasn't just a case of 'this is how things have always been done'. To them, kicking and punching people was the best bit of the job. And so I was genuinely pleased to see justice being done. After having seen so much that had been wrong, there was something very satisfying about seeing something that was right for once. And the fact that it had been done in front of us, adding to Rat boy's shame, made it all the more worthwhile.

After passing on a few words of advice, Dias released his grip, leaving Rat boy to dust himself off and scurry away.

Twenty-four hours later, after being upgraded to a coach for the short journey from Castel to the train station, we were on a train heading back to Marseilles. This time though, we no longer had to ask permission to go to the toilet and sat ourselves down in the buffet carriage and ordered a drink.

It might not have sounded much, but this was our first taste of civilisation in nearly five months and it felt incredible.

Besides....if the stories about the REP were true, it might be my last for quite a while!

Legion Para

As we sat at the end of the runway, the engines of the Transal transport plane started to roar causing the whole plane to vibrate and shake so much it seemed a miracle it remained in one piece. The brakes were finally released and in practically no time at all we were airborne, climbing steeply into the sunny Mediterranean sky towards Corsica, a hundred miles or so off the French coast.

We had been separated from our fellow recruits when we'd reached Marseille and our numbers had been increased to ten with Legionnaires from other regiments who had volunteered and been accepted for parachute training. We had been collected by a Sergeant from the REP who was escorting us back to Corsica and he sat quietly in the canvas seats of the Transal, engrossed in his newspaper and only engaging with us it seemed in sign language to motion 'go here,' 'sit there' or 'do that.' It reminded me of the way Dias had been and looking around at the other volunteers, they all looked as apprehensive as I did, which considering some had two or three years' service I found comforting that I was not on my own. This was the reputation the REP had, even amongst Legionnaires from other regiments and it got me thinking that coming straight from basic training probably put myself, Buchy and Didier at an advantage. We didn't have the skills or the experience for sure, but then we were still in that basic training mind-set and didn't have another regiment to compare things to.

We were told that the REP was still the only regiment that had evening and morning *appel* every day. In that respect it was just like basic training and even at the weekend, it you wanted to be excused evening *appel* and go out on town, then a pass, signed by the company commander was needed, but you still had to be back for

morning *appel* on Sunday. This differed from all other regiments in
the Legion, where you could get weekend passes so that you didn't
have to be back until Monday morning having spent the weekend
in Paris. Added to this restriction was that even when allowed out,
permission was only ever granted to visit the local town of Calvi,
and with uniforms having to be worn at all times, the bars and
restaurants in town were full of paratroopers. But with the military
police also constantly patrolling the town centre, most of the time
it just felt like an extension of the barracks.

Those joys though were still a month away and as the tailgate
opened and we walked onto the tarmac we were greeted by a
blast of hot air. I could see the heat hazes rippling up from the
runway, and looking out I could see the Corsican Mountains
climbing high into the distance. They looked like a patchwork of
greeny brown gorse bushes that covered the grey rocks that occasionally poked though in little outcrops. The two-hour journey
from Bastia Airport to Camp Raffalli gave us a close-up at this for-
midable looking terrain, where the only flat bits of the island
seemed to be around the coastline, because as soon as you were
a couple of kilometres inland the mountains rose up steeply, and
we were soon into narrow twisty roads that made it impossible to
get any real speed up. Small bits of the landscape had been flattened in order to be farmed, and the views across the valleys and
the tall stone bridges that crossed the flowing river gorges were
truly breathtaking. Pleasant as they were to look at though, as a
soldier I knew that stomping across them in this heat laden down
like a pack mule was going to be exhausting and I wondered how
I'd cope.

As we passed over a crescent in the road I could see the bay of
Calvi stretching out to our right, looking like a picture taken from
a travel brochure with its curved golden beaches and inviting blue
sea. Camp Raffalli itself is located just on the outskirts of Calvi,
about 500m from the seafront and is an immaculate collection of
whitewashed buildings, painted curb stones and polished brass
signs. The parade square greets you as you pass the main gate and
the peak of Monte Cinto that reaches over 3000m above sea level

dominates the backdrop. In mountain terms, that's about twice the height of Ben Nevis and most Legionnaires will make at least one trip to the top before they leave.

Our accommodation was a rather pleasant looking single story building that would house us during our parachute training. But surprisingly there was no permanent training staff, as each group, or PROMO as it was called was instructed by whichever qualified Sergeant Chef and accompanying corporal were available at the time.

The Regiment we were told, was split into four combat companies, each with its own speciality. And there was also a fire support company that consisted of a heavy mortars platoon, two MILAN anti-tank platoons, a reconnaissance platoon and the regiment's pathfinder, or Special Forces platoon. As the regiment was completely self sufficient, there was also a mechanics company to look after all the vehicles, and an HQ company that provided all the support staff, like the cooks, drivers, admin staff, medics etc. But these latter two companies were not available to new Legionnaires.

Most of the newly 'winged' Legionnaires would end up in one of the four infantry companies and would specialise in either urban warfare, mountain warfare, amphibious warfare, or train as a sniper and demolitions expert. As our instructors were from the 2nd Company (mountain warfare) we were told that more than likely, that would be our destination. Most of the new recruits though, myself included, fancied the amphibious warfare company, because with their own centre located right on the beach front, the thought of playing around in inflatable dinghys in the Meddy during the summer sounded superb....especially after months of basic training. And so reports that it was one of the toughest courses around were not unsurprisingly falling on deaf ears....as if?....all that sun and sand sounds like a real hardship!

The days here were hot and long and started each morning with a run which made the morning runs in Castel seem like a casual jog. The Drop Zone (DZ) was right next to the camp and whole area was surrounded by a horseshoe of mountains, so that within ten minutes of running out of the back gate we found ourselves running uphill, trying to keep up with the Chef whose long legs seemed to take one step for every two of mine. The sun was hot even at 8 o'clock in the morning and I was drenched in sweat by the time we'd reached the small village of Lumio which looked down on the camp, before we descended back through the rocky outcrops and arrived at the beach for the final leg home. The soft sand sapped the last of the strength from my legs and by the time we'd reached our billet, I was barely capable of standing still and listening to the Chef without collapsing into a heap on the floor. This was in stark contrast to the Chef himself, who had a North African complexion and didn't even seem to be out of breath as he explained that the next three weeks would be all about two things....and two things only. Building up our fitness, (which was nowhere near the standard required if today's run was anything to go by) and teaching us about military parachuting. During the fourth week we would need to make six jumps to qualify for our wings, one of them being at night!!

This pretty much set the standard for how are days were. After our morning PT which was always an hour long sprint into the mountains and back, the morning would be spent on the edge of the DZ practicing everything we needed to know about parachuting. From how to exit the aircraft properly to what to do if there is a problem with the chute in the air, and how to land correctly so as to avoid injury. In contrast to all previous training in the Legion, I found this was a relatively calm affair. And both the Chef and the Corporal, although strict, were keen to ensure that we understood every single detail and drill, pushing us to repeat them over and over until they became second nature.

The training facility was also excellent and there was even the fuselage of a Transal that had crashed into the side of a mountain (not exactly what we wanted to hear) and had been collected piece by piece and reassembled, complete with the interior. The chutes that we used were static line round chutes that opened automatically as we exited the aircraft and could be steered forwards, backwards, left and right by way of four cords that opened and closed windows in the chute. Although steering was forbidden except in the event of a collision, which apparently was a common occurrence, because on an average pass thirty Legionnaires would exit the aircraft in about seven or eight seconds.

In the afternoons we would continue with our parachute training and then finish the day with more sport, leaving just enough time for a shower before dinner. And in the evenings we were put to work usually weeding the small garden or painting something, before being given an hour or so free time before lights out. The foyer (Legionnaire's shop on site) was out of bounds and although the PROMO was physically knackering, it was conducted in a fairly relaxed atmosphere. And with enough food and water I could feel my fitness increasing so that when during the third week we were told we'd be running in full kit, I wasn't too concerned.

The 8km run in full kit, which we'd done once at Castel, was a standard test in the Legion, and had a maximum time allowance of one hour. Anything more would be considered physically substandard, but not surprisingly the REP had its own time allowances. They also had their own route, which instead of being on a flat tarmac road as in Castel, was twice around the DZ. This was an oblong shape with a constant uphill gradient running from one end to the other. Fit blokes would finish in around 35 minutes and anything over fifty would be tantamount to signing your own death warrant.

We assembled at 6am due to the heat, and with our rucksacks weighed in at 12 kg set off at our own pace. Didier as usual was off like a racing snake, and although I started off well, the long gentle climb up the back length of the DZ soon began to drain my strength, so that by the time I'd completed the first lap I was already done in. The second lap seemed to last forever and I finally crossed the finish line in 43 minutes in about 4th or 5th place, gasping for a drink and feeling a little light headed. This effort though was considered no more than a very average time, but our numbers had already dwindled as one of the PROMO had collapsed with heat stroke and was at present in the infirmary, covered in ice, where once recovered he would be given one more chance with the next PROMO before being rejected by the regiment.

As for us though, our parachute training was all but over and I just hoped that I hadn't forgotten anything.

On the morning of our first jump we were up early and there was an air of underlying tension that was showing through however well we tried to cover it up. Buchy was chain smoking and Didier wouldn't shut up, whilst I was like a nervous traveller who kept checking for their passport every five seconds and couldn't stop messing with my kit.

We were scheduled for three jumps, one with no kit, the second with no kit but we would deploy our reserve chute whilst in the air, and a third with our rucksacks wrapped in a thick canvas bag, which was secured to the front of our legs and then released in the air, where it would dangle beneath on a 6-metre cord. And it was this bag that I kept checking to disguise my anxiety. I just wanted to get going, but by the time we'd arrived at the airport, there were already Legionnaires from the combat companies being issued with their parachutes and lining up in the order they would be jumping in.

The PROMO 'stick' always jumped first and always on its own to give it as much 'clean air' as possible. We would all get a chance to be the first one out, but the Chef volunteered yours truly to be the first up. I tried to convince myself that ignorance was bliss and so better to get it over and done with. I ran through my pre-jump checks, that we all carried out before boarding, but messed up most of them and was pulled out by the jump master for a number of errors (as were most of the PROMO). This was met by jeers from the other Legionnaires who continued to take the piss as we made our way to the rear of the Transal, where the sickly smell of aviation fuel filled the air as we struggled to climb up the tailgate. Those who had rucksacks strapped to their legs could only manage a sort of slow waddle and had to be helped in by the person in front. Being the first out I was the last one to board and by the time I'd clambered aboard, the plane was packed with paratroopers jammed into their seats so tightly that it was impossible for the load masters to make their way down the aircraft, and they were forced to walk over the top of people.

I was already sweating as we waited on the runway when there was a tap on my shoulder as Buchy handed me my 'clip', which I would attach to the steel wire that ran down the length of the aircraft, ensuring that my chute would automatically deploy. The clip was kept on the side of my chute, but as we were packed in like sardines, you could only reach the guy's in front of you and I gave him the thumbs up as the electric motors started to whine, closing the tailgate and shutting out the outside world. Next time I'd see daylight, I'd hopefully be floating gently towards the ground, and with the temperature starting to rise inside, the air felt heavy and hot as the aircraft rocked back and forth under the power of the engines before the brakes were released. The steep climb was over in no time as the aircraft levelled off out at sea, before making a sweeping turn and heading back inland. I could see liquid running under the steel grates in the floor, which didn't seem to be right, and thought that maybe it would be better to jump out after all.

The load master was chatting on his intercom and I could feel a knot in my stomach like I'd never felt before. Looking back down the plane, Buchy had gone a very pale colour and I wondered whether I looked the same, whilst further down the line, Legionnaires were chatting away like they were on a sightseeing bus. I guess this is what was meant as being 'green,' in more ways than one, and the heat wasn't helping as I dried the palms of my hands once more on my pants.

The plane's steep climb from the runway was over in seconds before it started to bank sharply. The load master then made a gesture and the side doors of the aircraft opened, letting in a sudden blast of cool air and making it impossible to hear anything. Looking down the line, the PROMO was gestured to 'stand up' and 'hook on,' and after passing down the line checking we'd done so, the load master pointed at me to move forward towards the door.

I could see the sea below us when the Chef positioned me in the doorway. I had one foot forward and my hands either side of the door to catapult myself into thin air. The noise of the engine only a few feet away suddenly dropped, slowing us down to our jump speed. I concentrated hard and tried to remember the drill for being number one in the stick. Unlike in the movies there was no red and green light, but there were two signals to jump. The first was a loud buzzer and the second was a gentle shove by the load master, just in case you had second thoughts. And I was wondering whether I *was* going to have second thoughts and freeze in the doorway, when the world slipped from beneath me.

I don't know whether I jumped or whether I was pushed, but half a second later it felt like I was inside a washing machine. I was completely helpless for a few more seconds until it seemed as though someone had gently picked me up by the shoulders and I realised I was stationary in the air. I checked my chute as instructed, but never having seen one from this angle before, I guessed it seemed OK and so looked around for the rest of the PROMO. The complete silence suddenly seemed so peaceful and I had the most amazing view of the DZ with the camp away to my right and Calvi in the distance. But this serenity only lasted a few seconds as I noticed the ground getting closer and braced myself into the drop position. The ground arrived with a huge thump that knocked the wind out of me and by the time I'd started to collect my chute together, the sky was full of Legionnaires from the second drop. After stuffing my chute back into its pouch, I threw it on my back and sprinted to the regrouping point and twenty minutes later we were back at the airport for our second jump of the day. Everyone had made a successful jump and with the adrenaline still pumping, we were re-telling our own experiences as we boarded the plane and made our way to the back, because this time around we would be the last stick out.

It was a great experience seeing the other sticks jump and some of them wailed like Banshees as they exited. And I could even hear one of the French loadmasters shouting in English

'GO! GO! GO!'

The second jump was fantastic. This time we opened out reserve chutes whilst in the air and floated down under two canopies, landing almost without falling over. The third jump of the day also went well, and we all managed to make it back to barracks with no more than a few bruises between us. That is apart from Buchy, who hadn't held his helmet down on exit and the g-force caused when the chute opens was so great, that the straps on the helmet cut like a razor blade under his ears. And so by the time the medics had finished he looked like he was wearing a pair of headphones.

Over the next two days we completed the final three jumps needed to qualify as paratroopers. And a day later, during a very proud ceremony we were issued with our wings and the insignia of the regiment. In many ways, being accepted into the REP was a prouder moment for me than getting my Kepi. It was difficult to put into words how it felt just to have made it this far, but earning my wings made me feel both 'a bit different', and 'a bit special' at the same time.

These moments though as always in the Legion were short-lived and there was always someone more than willing not to let you enjoy life too much and bring you back down to earth (normally with a huge bang thrown in for good measure). Ours came when we were told that we would no longer be going to the 2nd Company as there was a greater need in the Fire Support Company (known as the CEA). Or to be more precise everyone apart from Didier, Buchy and I would still be going to 2nd Company. Having already got used to the idea of going to 2nd Company and even been introduced and shown around, it just seemed like another Legion way of keeping you guessing and pissing you off. We would also be leaving the rest of the PROMO whom we'd developed a real bond with over the last month. And although still in the same regiment, we new that with the intensity of training and the fact that the companies were often on overseas tours at different times, it meant that we may not see each other again for quite some time.

On the up side though the CEA was housed over on the far side of the camp and slightly away from the combat companies. It was a modern 'H' shaped building that reminded me of the similarly named notorious prison in Northern Ireland. Entering the Captain's office one by one, we were at least relieved to find out we would be staying together and going to the Milan Platoon. This was the anti-tank platoon, who were not in barracks at present because they had just started their annual training course that was designed for both Legionnaires and newly promoted Corporals. But they were sending a jeep to pick us up after lunch and there was a Corporal already waiting upstairs.

It all seemed like yet another whirlwind as we struggled with all our gear up the stairs, only to be greeted by a corporal who looked like a gorilla with a deformed head. It was unusually large and his big dopey eyes gave him the same blank expression as a cow. After grunting out a few incoherent orders, he gave us a brush and mop and told us to get going on the corridor and showers. Didier tried explaining we'd been told there was a jeep on its way, but that didn't seem to register and he disappeared back into his room leaving us to scrub the floor. Half an hour later the jeep duly arrived with another corporal, who immediately started gobbing off at 'Cowhead' because we were not ready. But Cowhead's response was to simply grab Didier by the throat and demand to know why he'd not said anything. Didier though, already starting to wise up, kept his mouth shut and just apologised for not speaking out.

Pissed off, the second corporal who introduced himself as 'Rocky', (although this was due to the similarity of his name rather than anything to do with boxing), rummaged though the store-room throwing bits of kit at us until we had what we needed. Including a civilian rucksack, which the regiment had bought because they considered the French Army ones useless.

Stuffed into the back of the jeep we sped off back down the coast road for a half an hour, passing tourists who were enjoying the scorching August sunshine, until turning inland and heading up mountain roads, eventually making our way down the side of a reservoir. Our camp was located at the far end and the tents had been arranged around a small square that had been cleared away. Rocks, painted white had then been placed in perfectly straight lines around the edge to create a sort of mini parade square, complete with a flag pole that was flying the French Tricolour. And in the baking heat it looked like the little outposts in the dessert that had always been synonymous with the Legion.

Sitting in a chair, relaxing in the sun with his top off was the senior sergeant and we immediately snapped to attention as he shaded his eyes from the sun to get a better look at us. His torso was wiry looking like a lightweight boxer's, and when he stood up you could see a tattoo of Jesus being crucified on the cross that covered his chest and stomach, giving him that slightly psychotic look that immediately put you on edge. He was French, and introduced himself as Sergeant Moreau, before explaining that the platoon commander wanted to see us.

Unlike most platoons, ours was commanded by an NCO who had joined as a Legionnaire and risen up through the ranks until reaching the rank of Adjutant, which in the French Army is the equivalent to Sergeant Major. On entering his tent I came to attention and gave him my best presentation in full, but he seemed unimpressed and just continued reading, not even bothering to look up from his desk. I was wandering if he'd even heard me, when he suddenly sprang out of his chair, and stopping just in front of me, placed his hand out gesturing for me to shake.

'Welcome to the Milan Platoon!' he said, incredibly cheerfully.

Although a little surprised by this familiarity, I had noticed that at morning parade, the corporals and sergeants in the Legion always shook hands. And so presuming this was just a formality, reached out to return the gesture. But at the last second he pulled his hand back and swung it around, punching me in the mouth. I was stunned for a second until he grabbed my collar and told me never to shake the hand of an Adjutant again. This was then followed by some more abuse about me being a worthless piece of shit before I was finally thrown out of the tent. Landing on the floor, I looked up to see the smiling face of Rocky, who was obviously in on the whole joke, and dusting myself off could only raise a frown at Buchy who looked like he was about to enter a lion's den, as he pulled back the flaps on the tent and nervously went in. Two minutes later he came hurtling out, leaving poor old Didier the last one to enter.

'Did he get you with the handshake thing?'

'Yeah…thinks he's a real comedian doesn't he?'

An hour or so later, after having cleaned up the small kitchen area, the three of us were introduced to the Milan Anti Weapon that was going to be the tool of our trade in the regiment. Having missed a day or so of the course, the afternoon was spent with Sergeant Moreau, whose crash lesson mostly consisted of us sprinting up and down the sides of a quarry and setting up the anti-tank weapon in makeshift firing positions. The firing post weighed 16kg and sprinting up the steep sides of the quarry with it balanced on your shoulders, through the loose rocks that gave way under your feet, was like wading through quicksand. The heat of the mid afternoon sapped my energy, but you couldn't afford to just throw the Milan around as the optic system made it fairly fragile. But after an hour or so of this punishment we were finally allowed to rest. From the shade of a large boulder, Moreau explained that the Milan was a wire guided anti-tank system that fired a shaped charge. It could be guided whilst still in flight by way of electrical signals that were passed down a thin wire that trailed behind the missile. He told us that it could stop most modern tanks. The course we were on would last five weeks and would culminate in a live fire exercise in mainland France.

I knew that the British Army also used the Milan and it was highly respected by the infantry, due to a combination of its portability, accuracy and destructive power. And with recent improvements, it was now even capable of punching through the most modern of armour plating. Moreau explained that we would become experts in all aspects of the Milan, including how to use the weapon at platoon and regimental level. The platoon was also equipped with jeeps, fitted with special mountings for the Milan. But for the time being it was all about carrying them on your back.

Despite my first impression, Moreau seemed a reasonably fair bloke and in this place that was about the best you could hope for. I had quickly learnt to distinguish between those who were tough taskmasters and those who were simply cruel bastards. And the longer I was here, the easier they became to spot. Some people like Cowhead and Rocky, before they even opened their mouths, you could tell were evil, enjoying the control and power that rank gave them, rather than the challenge of leading soldiers. With people like Moreau though, they might not exactly be the type of people you would take home to meet your mother, but at least most of the time you knew where you stood with them. It was strange, because he may have only run us ragged all afternoon in the baking sun, but I already trusted him!

The next two days were spent doing much of the same and the evenings spent either practising with the thermal sight, that was so accurate it could pick up the heat signature of rabbits running across the fields in the dead of night, or learning to identify most of the tanks and armoured vehicles in world, from photographs taken at awkward angles. We also met the rest of the platoon where I was assigned to Moreau's team, which consisted of Rocky, another corporal called Valera and four other Legionnaires including myself.

Valera, from Madrid, seemed pretty laid back and had only just completed his corporal's school. The rest of the team consisted of Fino, who was from Italy, Ducs from Poland, both of whom had been Officers in the army, and Jacques, a quietly spoken Frenchman from Normandy who had been a Sergeant in the French regulars.

With the exception of Rocky they all seemed like good lads and accepted me straight away without question or judgement. And it was as this group that we lined up early next morning in preparation for the march back to Calvi, which was going to mean ignoring the roads and going in a straight line, over the mountains. I tried not to show my nervousness as we collected our gear together and I wondered what the next few hours would hold. How fast would we be marching? How far and how long would it take us? These questions and more were buzzing around my mind when I was given a missile filled with concrete and told to strap it to my rucksack. I wanted to do well on my first march to be accepted by the section. I'd had my difficulties with marching at Castel and there was no way I wanted to embarrass myself here. But that suddenly seemed the least of my worries when I felt the weight of the missile. It was basically the plastic cover of a missile that had already been fired and then filled with concrete to simulate the same weight of 12kg. It looked like a drainpipe and was about five foot long and hung out on each side of my rucksack once strapped horizontally to the top, which would have been fine if someone hadn't poured all the concrete into one end, so that when I stood up it was virtually impossible to stand straight without falling over to one side. Fino on the other hand, being a devious bastard had gotten up early and bagged the lightest missile he could lay his hands on, whilst Ducs and Jacques would be carrying a firing post each.

We set off with Moreau in front and started back down the side of the reservoir for a kilometre or so before climbing over an old dry stone wall and heading straight up the side of a steep hill. Ducs was in front of me and I could see him sifting the firing post around trying to make it more comfortable. He was well over six foot and well built, but as the steepness of the hill took its toll he started to swear in Polish which Rocky responded to in their native tongue. In Castel speaking your own language was an absolute forbidden, but Moreau didn't seem to care as he carried on with his blistering pace, adjusting his beret so that it was perched rather casually on the back of his head and looked more like a Jewish skull cap.

The pace was ferocious and the combination of the heat and my lopsided rucksack was absolutely exhausting. It was difficult to walk in a straight line and I was constantly shifting from side to side in an attempt to get the weight central as we crested the hill and found ourselves on a short stretch of flat ground. We had been going less than an hour and I was already dead on my feet when Moreau turned and made a wisecrack about the 'warm up' being over and to get ready for the real march. I was hoping he was joking when he turned and asked how the 'Anglais' was coping, to which Rocky replied that he didn't care as long as I kept going. Half an hour later when we stopped for a breather, I slumped down on the floor and started gulping down the contents of my water bottle. I could see that Rocky was getting something out of his rucksack and apart from a lightweight sleeping bag it was completely empty. The bastard must have emptied most of his stuff out into the trucks, and I later learned that so had Fino and Valera. Only Ducs and Jacques hadn't, because it was impossible to balance the firing post on top of an empty rucksack.

'How's your rucksack Anglais? Not too heavy I hope?'

Through gritted teeth I smiled back at Moreau and tried to make out I didn't care. They must have been laughing all the way because they knew my rucksack was filled with everything from spare boots, extra clothing and even a fleece jacket. Not having been issued with a locker at Calvi, Rocky had insisted we bring all our gear with us.

Starting off again the terrain became more barren, but moving carefully along goat paths we made our way through the rocky mountainside. The paths were sided with a sort of thick gorse bush that had spread everywhere, covering up most of the rock, and I found the missile constantly getting snagged in its branches. Once stuck, I would have to pull like mad until it suddenly gave way and I'd end up popping out of the other side like a champagne cork. It also left a sticky brownish resin on whatever it touched, and mixed with sweat I literally looked like I'd been dragged through the proverbial hedge backwards by the time it had thinned out enough for me to walk unhindered.

This was what was called 'Maquis' and it covered huge areas of the mountainside and made marching twice as difficult, but after a monumental effort climbing up another hill, I could finally see the bay of Calvi and our camp away in the distance. It was a wonderful sight that lifted my morale, but as we started our precarious descent, the steep unmade paths kept giving way under our top-heavy packs and more than once Ducs lost his balance, only to be met by a torrent of abuse by Moreau. Dropping the Milan down the side of a mountain was certainly not going to win him any prizes and by the time we'd reached firmer ground, there wasn't a Polish swear word I didn't know.

The shade provided by the narrow village backstreets of Lumio felt refreshing, and benefiting from the cooling breeze, we stopped to sort ourselves out. A local man passed us by in the street and didn't even raise a glance as we straightened out our uniform before starting the last leg of the march back to camp. We entered through the back gate and set about unloading the trucks that had already arrived whilst Moreau supped on an ice cold beer, controlling which bits of kit went where.

The march had taken no more than three hours or so and although carrying more gear than some, I really don't think I could have taken one more step. And I was beginning to think that coming to the 'Rep' might not have been such a good idea after all.

March or Die

My head had fallen forward under the weight of my helmet and I found it impossible to muster enough energy to lift it back up in order to take a decent lungfull of air. Staring at my feet I could clearly see that my boots were coated in the light brown dust that was being kicked up as we ran down the back of the DZ, but the sound of people shouting at me had become almost muted. I could occasionally make out my name, but for the most part in was just an inaudible noise. My feet had been numb for the last twenty minutes and with my head slumped, I knew that I wouldn't last much longer.

It was a horrible and rather strange feeling knowing that your body was running on reserve and that you were completely helpless to stop it from breaking down. It almost felt like being trapped inside a car that was heading towards a cliff in slow motion, knowing that the brakes and steering had failed, but still frantically trying to wrestle with the controls to stop the inevitable from happening.

I knew that the 8km run in full kit would be hard, but carrying the Milan firing post as well, in the scorching afternoon heat, was just insane. And as we passed the ambulance that was on standby, I tried hard just to concentrate on putting one foot in front of the other to keep the momentum going. Fino was next to me and was already being pushed along by Rocky and Ducs who were running with just the added burden of a missile each. Maybe Jacques and Valera were also pushing me, but I felt so far gone I couldn't really tell, and besides, thinking about it was proving too tiring. In fact I couldn't really think straight about anything and even raising my hand to wipe the sweat out of my eyes seemed out of the question. I had one hand on the leg of the Milan to hold it on top of my rucksack, and the other I was trying to swing furiously back and forth like a sort of pendulum in a vain attempt to throw my body weight forward with each step. By half way around the second lap I could feel my body begin to give in and each time it did, I shouted at myself to keep going. I could feel myself fade a little more with each step, until I was running on 'autopilot' and no longer seemed to have any control over my arms and legs. It felt like my body had decided to take over and was ignoring any instructions I gave it. And with my head slumped forward and unable to breath properly, I knew that however much I protested, going down was only a matter of time,…….. when my head was suddenly wrenched up and I could hear Moreau screaming in my ear:

'BREATHE….and don't drop that fuckin' Milan!'

His fingers were locked under the lip of my helmet and I gulped down some air as he dragged me along and poured my water bottle over my neck.

'Nobody stops until I say!'

With my head back up though, I knew that we still had a kilometre or so to go. But with the lads pushing and Moreau pulling we eventually passed the finish line, where we were allowed to collapse in the shade of the ambulance that was now handing out bottles of water….where we stayed, unable to speak for next ten minutes.

We had completed the 8km run in 50 minutes in the middle of the afternoon in August, carrying full kit and the Milan.

After sprinting back to our rooms to change and shower for the next lesson that was about to start, I quickly starting pulling off my boots, when Tinc, a small Turkish Legionnaire that was also on the Milan course, sat down on his bed and just suddenly collapsed.

I was taken aback at first as he had seemed fine just a second ago, and although guessing that it was probably heat stroke, didn't really know what to do. I knew that heat stroke could be a killer and that when the body's core temperature gets too much, it simply shuts down everything it considers unnecessary for survival, like Tinc's consciousness, and I also new that time was imperative so I shouted out for the platoon medic.

Jim, who was a corporal and one of the few English speaking Legionnaires in the platoon, had recently trained for four months in France to qualify as the medic. Grabbing his bag, a group of us carried Tinc outside and placed him, or rather dumped him under a bank of taps that we normally used to clean our boots. He was still unconscious as Jim wrapped a rubber band around his bicep, rubbing alcohol on his arm and slapping at the skin to try and get a vein up, before he managed to push a drip in, holding it all in place with a bit of tape and stabilising his condition before taking him to the Infirmary.

Jim's knowledge and skill was incredibly impressive and much greater than I'd expected at platoon level. Over a beer later that day he explained that to qualify as the platoon medic you had to complete a 16-week intensive programme that consisted of lectures, as well as hands-on experience, going on call out with the Ambulance crews and spending time in the A&E department of Toulouse Hospital. It sounded like an excellent course and very professionally run, where they learnt everything from stitching people up to how to give a simple flu jab. Given the way he'd dealt with Tinc and the number of people that were dropping out, it was comforting to know that he was looking after us if anything went wrong. Collapsing in the barracks with heat stroke was one thing, but in the mountains it would be quite another.

The incredible pace continued over the next month through the heat of August with absolutely no let up; lessons every evening and even at the weekends, although Sunday afternoon was given over to cleaning your own kit. Unless of course you were new, which meant you would spend that time cleaning the platoon's gear and your own kit would have to wait. It was bizarre really, because I'd been in the Legion a little over seven months now and the most relaxed we'd been was during the parachute training, which according to the stories whilst at Castel should have been the hardest thing we'd ever have to do during our five years. To be honest, right now it seemed like a relaxing month in the sun compared to this. We were though pretty much left alone by the corporals in the platoon, who had a fearsome reputation for giving the new lads a horrendous time. Even Jim had said that normally a new Legionnaire's life was hell for the first couple of months and that we'd only gotten a little taster of it when we'd first met the Adjutant. The fact that the corporals were involved in the Milan course as well, which meant there was literally no time left in the day to mess us around, was, according to Jim, a bit of a godsend.

Funny though....it just didn't seem that running or marching everywhere with a Milan strapped to your back could be described in any way as 'a good deal!'

Still....what did I know! As far as the rest of the platoon was concerned I'd only just arrived. Even during the Milan course, I'd noticed that although we were singled out for every shitty job going (a pastime that the Legion was second to none at creating), it was only those Legionnaires with more than two years' service that actually seemed to have things a bit easier. Everyone else was treated as completely worthless.

There was an enormous amount of information to take in and remember on the course, including loads of stuff that was obviously useful, like being able to identify an enemy tank in poor light from only a brief glimpse of the barrel, to things that seemed a bit pointless, like being able to name every single component of the missile and even the type of metal that made up the shaped charge. Not that we would ever see a missile though, because they were fitted to the firing post in their plastic tubes which had the ends sealed up. It seemed that no technical detail was omitted so that after a month of the same, I was sure if asked, we could have made our own Milan from a few old toilet rolls and a bit of string.

One lesson that was important though and taught over and over was how to deploy with the Milan as paratroopers. During the PROMO I'd seen the Mortar platoon jump with their kit, throwing it out first under its own parachutes. The Milan could also be deployed in the same way, by being strapped to a square piece of wood that had shopping trolley wheels on it so that it could be manoeuvred inside the aircraft. The missiles, in packs of four, were deployed in a similar fashion, straight after the firing post, each being pushed and then followed by a Legionnaire. The load masters in the aircraft were apparently insistent that the Legionnaires jumped out practically holding onto them, but given that in their packaging they weighed well over 70kg, the unwritten rule amongst the Legionnaires was to push the gear, wait half a second and then follow. That would give you a good 20 metres or so of clean air. The last thing you wanted was to get hit by a 70kg dead weight travelling at 100 miles an hour.

And all this training was put into practice a week later when we put on a display for the Defence Minister who was visiting Corsica.

The plan was to exit the plane in 'sticks' with the Milan, grab the gear and then run 500 metres or so to set up in a firing position inside a protective parameter, which would be provided by the reconnaissance platoon, who would be jumping with their heavy calibre half-inch Browning machine guns. It sounded quite simple in theory and would be watched by a crowd of dignitaries, who were to be seated on a platform on the side of the drop zone. The practices went well, but jumping with the platoon for the first time was quite nerve-wracking as I didn't want to mess up in any way. I was to be jumping last and on hitting the ground would ditch my chute, sprint over to the missiles, grab one and make my way to the re-grouping position.

As the aircraft made its sweeping turn over the bay we were up almost immediately, hooking on and making our final checks. Ducs was already in the door ready to push the firing post, to be followed by Jacques with the second. Rocky and Valera would be next out, quickly trailed by Fino with the missiles, then Moreau and finally yours truly. Arguably Jacques and Fino had the most difficult jobs as they had to try and manoeuvre their 70kg trolley forward, which was no easy task inside a shaking steel tube, then turn 90 degrees towards the door and get out. Given that at 100 miles an hour the plane was travelling at around 40-50 metres a second, speed was absolutely crucial and looking forward I realised that as last man out, I was probably in the peach position. I might have a little further to run once on the ground, but that was all.

As we waited for the buzzer to sound, I knew that the reconnaissance platoon would already be on the ground, having dropped during the first pass. The load master took his arm from in front of Ducs that was acting as a sort of barrier between him and fresh air

and placed it on his shoulder. The buzzer rang out and the butterflies disappeared as we all started pushing forward into each other
as if in a queue that wasn't moving fast enough. I could hear the
load master shouting as he dragged at Jacques' trolley to get it out
as fast as possible. It seemed to get stuck for a second but after a
huge push it suddenly came free and flew out of the door, causing
Jacques to loose his footing and fall forward, still three or four feet
back from the door. He was literally horizontal as his top half got
caught in the airflow and sucked him out of the aircraft head first.
The last thing I saw was a pair of boots, three feet off the ground
flying forward and exiting the plane. It was absolutely hilarious and
I only hoped that it was no more than his pride that had taken a
battering. But as my chute popped open and I looked around to get
my bearings, I realised I had problems all of my own. It was
normally pretty easy to recognise the DZ, but as I looked down, all
I could make out were a few trees and a tarmac road. I panicked for
a second and then looked further out and finally recognised on old
tank in front of me that I knew was at one end of the DZ. That
meant I had over-shot the DZ by at least three or four hundred
metres, and looking down I could see lines of dry stone walls loom-
ing up at me like a spider's web. I pulled hard on the direction lines
and the chute swung to the right. I braced myself as I glided over
the top of one wall and landed on a dirt track in front of the
entrance to a small farm.

I counted my blessings for having landed in one piece and
collecting my chute, suddenly felt very alone. I couldn't see anyone
and not wanting to just leave my chute as instructed, started
making my way back to the DZ when I heard my name being called
out from above. Moreau had landed in a tree on the edge of the DZ
and was suspended ten feet above the ground hanging on the main
trunk. But pulling at the straps, he broke free and managed to lower
himself to the ground.

I'd heard of the SAS practising parachuting into trees in the
1950's or 1960's, but had given up due to the high number of
injuries sustained, so I was thinking how lucky he was to still be in
one piece. We made our way over the barbed wire fence at the back

of the DZ, where we saw the missile trolley laying next to the old tank, with the lid already off. This was a good sign as someone had already got there and made off with their load, but as I dragged the missiles out, I noticed there were still three left, but before I had time to even pose the question, Moreau looked down at me.

'Take two'

'Bollocks'

They had been made extra heavy as Moreau had wanted to impress the defence Minister if he came around, and as the re-grouping point was a couple of kilometres away at the other end of the DZ, I knew the run wasn't going to be pleasant.

Twenty minutes later and probably a good half-hour after we'd first made our jump, myself and Moreau finally arrived at the re-grouping point. We were met with a torrent of abuse from the Corporals who had mistaken Moreau for a Legionnaire because he was carrying a missile. And it was quite satisfying watching them grovelling, once they'd realised their mistake, for having called him a 'lazy wanker'. But there was no time for a post-mortem of the events, and we made our way towards the firing position and the Defence Minister, who was by now probably bored senseless after having watched two lone figures making their way slowly down the DZ laden down with the world's heaviest drainpipes.

Probably not the slick show he been told to expect from the finest regiment in the French Army!!!!

As a nice present though for the two people not picking up their missiles, we spent the entire evening on our hands and knees scrubbing the corridor and showers whilst the Corporals put their feet up and chilled out with a few beers. Even though the two who had not picked up their missiles were Rocky and Valera - both Corporals! Such is the mentality in the Legion.

A week later we were standing on the quayside at Bastia after a two-hour trip in the jeeps from Calvi, waiting to board the overnight ferry for the twelve-hour crossing to the mainland. It was great to be surrounded by civilians again and much as I enjoyed the Legion, it was an uncomfortable reminder that I'd not worn civilian cloths or even just wandered around the shops, without being in the constant glare of our instructors, for nearly eight months. And so there was an air of eager anticipation as we waited to board. Without even a day off since I'd joined, the boat journey would be as close as most of us got to free time; because once we'd loaded our gear in the hold, there was nothing to do until we docked in Marseille the following morning. It might just have been a twelve-hour inconvenience for most of the passengers as they towed their caravans back to France, but for us it was like an oasis of peaceful calm in our olive green world of screaming orders. And so once under way we stood on deck and watched Corsica slowly disappear into shadow as the sun passed behind its great peaks.

I know it sounds slightly pathetic in hindsight, but after eight months of being the lowest form of life in the Legion, it was amazing how much that little bit of freedom did to recharge the batteries. And after a plate of 'steak frites' and a carafe of red wine....we felt almost human again.

After docking in Marseille we headed east towards the town of Draguignan and the Plateau of Canjuers, which was a huge area controlled by the military, and was perfect for firing all sorts of heavy munitions including the Milan. Located at about a 1000 metres above sea level, this huge flat pancake was perfectly suited to its purpose, sharing its vastness with a just few wild boars, which although protected from being hunted, still kept a low profile.

Chilled by the cold wind that blew unchecked across the plateau and being more used to the baking heat of Corsica, we dug out our Gortex jackets. We'd stopped next to a concrete hard standing that was to be our home for the next week, whilst preparing for the live firing test that would mark the end of the Milan Course....and hopefully a let-up in the pace. For the next few days we laboured non stop, setting up our camp, again creating a parade square from rocks collected from the surrounding hills. Any spare time was given over to practising on the 'simulator,' which was a real firing post adjusted so that it fired a laser instead of a missile. It gave an instant 'hit' or 'miss' reading and was a very useful training tool.

In theory, to hit a moving vehicle with the Milan was relatively simple. All you had to do was keep the cross hairs on the target and the electronics would do the rest. But unfortunately, because the electrical signals were passed down a thin spool of wire that was trailed behind the missile, any sudden movement could cause it to snap. The skill therefore to firing the Milan, was to make all movements smooth and continuous. The 'simulator' allowed us to practice this skill and it was something that everyone took extremely seriously..................not least because anyone who missed would have Moreau to answer to. And embarrassing him in front of the French Army wouldn't exactly put him in the best of moods!!

In my naivety I had half expected just to turn up at the firing range, blast off a few missiles and get off. But being the REP and in full view of the French Army, we would be marching in from sixty kilometres after being dropped off back down in the valley. I would be carrying the Milan and after ditching all but the absolute necessities from my rucksack, carefully took the time to prepare my feet, taping up all the weak points that might rub over the next two days. It reminded me of the Kepi Blanc march and it would be the furthest I'd marched since joining the REP. This time though I was better prepared and experience had taught me exactly what I needed to pack and how to make myself as comfortable as possible. But even so after just half a day's march my back was killing me. The weight of the Milan on top of my rucksack was agony as we stomped our way though the steep forest tracks, which occasionally flattened out, but never crested any peaks. Ducs with the other Milan was not faring much better either, but as ever was jabbering on in Polish to Rocky, until even Moreau got hacked off and told them to speak French. Fino had been strategically harbouring an empty missile tube all week and within seconds of discovering he would not be carrying the firing post already had it strapped to his rucksack. As a result he seemed to be on a Sunday afternoon stroll and much as I was struggling with the Milan, I know I would have done the same thing in his place.

By late afternoon the ground began to flatten out and we seemed to have done most of the climbing. The forests began to disappear giving way to the thin grassy vegetation that covered the rock bed of the plateau floor. And when Moreau called a halt to the day, I quickly set up a makeshift basha and collapsed onto the floor. The march had taken it out of me and I really wasn't finding the marching any easier the longer I was in the Legion. I'd expected it to get easier and although I was sure that my fitness was improving month on month, the goalposts seemed to move further and further away. Marching wasn't like running until you were knackered, where your lungs felt like they were on fire and your leg muscles were screaming with the build up of acid. This was more of a slow beating that steadily wore you down, like someone constantly pressing on a painful bruise until you couldn't take it any more, and it became a massive mental challenge just to keep putting one foot in front of the other.

After pulling the worst guard shift of the night (which was a privilege always reserved for the lowest ranking Legionnaire), we set off the following morning and after making good progress across the plateau passing one firing range after another, we arrived at our destination and set about preparing the Milan, as Moreau went off to collect the 'live' missiles and distribute the targets.

The firing range was a well organised French army affair and we would be firing at different moving targets simultaneously, simulating an enemy tank attack that would be co-ordinated by Moreau, who would designate targets to either myself or Ducs as he saw fit. Each firing post would have either Rocky or Valera as the commander, a firer and a loader. This way the live fire would be a test for the whole group, rather than just the skill of the firer. I concentrated hard as I lay in position for the first time with a live missile locked in place and scanned the horizon for potential targets. The Milan can fire out to just less than 2 kilometres and as I cleaned the eyepiece from a build-up of condensation, I heard a shout of

'1600 METERS....DIRECTION 2 O'CLOCK....ENEMY TANK....MOVING LEFT TO RIGHT.

FIRE!'

With the adrenaline pumping, I set the cross hairs on the target and pressed the firing button which instantly sent an electrical charge to the missile. It exploded into life and set off down the range chasing its target.

I could see the heat trail of the missile in the bottom of the sight but ignored it and just kept following the target with the cross hairs as the missile seemed to take forever to cover the 1600 meters, before finally smashing into the target sending up huge wads of earth and rock. I felt relief more than excitement at hitting the target, but within seconds Fino was locking a second missile in place for me and I saw Ducs' missile go snaking down the range for about a 1000 metres, taking out a fast moving vehicle.

My second target came almost instantly and was only 600 metres away which the missiles reached almost as soon as I'd pressed the fire button. Ducs' second was also on target giving us a clean sweep, and a sense of relief washed over us knowing that we'd passed the firing phase of the Milan course.

It was a great feeling, but unfortunately one that was short-lived as the rest of the day was spent doing a round robin of tests which was a culmination of everything we had learnt over the last eight weeks, including knowledge of the Milan system, tank iden-tification, camouflage skills, mechanical knowledge so that we could repair the jeeps, communication skills using the latest digital radios that could change frequency up to 200 times a second in order to scramble a signal, as well as map reading and chemical warfare knowledge. Our fitness was also tested as we were timed on our speed covering the ground travelling between the individual stations.

This then was our test day and after getting back to camp and sorting ourselves out, I was starting to feel quite smug with myself after the day's events and was thinking about climbing into my sleeping bag for a well earned rest when I heard Moreau shouting from outside, where we paraded a few seconds later.

Earlier in the evening we had scoured the place for any bits of litter that might have been dropped, but on later inspection Moreau had discovered a single fag butt, which in our black-and-white world meant that we were not doing our jobs properly and neither were the Corporals. As punishment, he wanted us to dig a pit; 2 metres by 2 metres wide and 2 metres deep, just in order to bury the offending item. I had almost grown immune to this kind of bullshit and had long since given up trying to figure out any logic to half of our orders. In fact many of them where designed just to get under your skin and so thinking about them just added to the frustration.

No....the only way not to let all the nonsense get to you was to just accept it. Not always easy I'll admit. Especially when you've been awake for almost two days, just marched your arse off and the offending fag butt, which was French, had been found in a part of the camp we'd not been near. As no one smoked French cigarettes, you didn't have to be Sherlock Holmes to figure out that it probably belonged to some other French Army unit that had used the camp before us.

Even so, dwelling on things was never a good idea in the Legion and so without even a groan of disgruntlement, we picked up our spades and set about our task. In fact, for once it was nice to see the Corporals being punished as well instead of standing on the sidelines gobbing off. It was tough going though, hacking through the bedrock and more than one pickaxe handle was broken before we'd finally finished. After a further inspection from Moreau though, followed by a slightly comical burial ceremony conducted by one of the French Legionnaires who had partially trained as a Priest, we were finally finished. Or so we thought!

Because as ever in the Legion, just as you let yourself think that things are over, they never usually are.

Moreau now decided that we should erect a monument to our hard work and toil in the form of a pyramid, built out of rocks, again 2 metres by 2 metres wide and with the peak being 2 metres high. This time we spilt into teams, one group collecting rocks whilst the other built, and I was amazed how many rucksacks full of rock actually went into the construction which took us most of the night. But in a final show of defiance, we even took extra time to hollow out a small archway where we placed a lighted candle. It might not seem that much now, but taking the extra time to create that little arch was our way of sticking two fingers up at Moreau

I suppose we were trying to piss him off by saying 'That a simple pyramid might be good enough to pass your inspection! But that's not good enough for us.'

A childish gesture maybe! But in this place you were trodden on so often that even the hollow victories seemed worthwhile.

That said, I'm not sure that I actually learnt anything new that evening about not dropping litter, or that all orders should be carried out in full however small. If indeed that's what he was trying to teach us. Because the reality was; if you hadn't picked that much up already, you weren't going to start now.

But on future visits to Canjuers in the following years, I suppose I did come to look upon that pyramid with a certain sense of pride.

A sort of permanent reminder of what made the 2nd REP that little bit different.

Commando School

The icy wind of the French Pyrenees stung the side of my face as we drove through the gates of the old Napoleonic Fort that dominated the small town of Mont Louis. Less than five miles from the Spanish border and only 10 from Andorra, the fort had originally been built to protect France from British invasion from the south, but had since been converted into a Commando school.

It was late October and my hope of a slow down in the pace after the Milan course had been short-lived. After a couple of weeks of guard duties back in Corsica we were given orders that we would be attending the French Army Commando School and would be training hard in preparation.

A three week course, we would be learning everything from unarmed combat to how to blow up radio masts and the like. All in all it sounded like excellent fun and much as I knew it would be hard work, I was really looking forward to it and as a platoon we set about training almost immediately. But there was also another upside to being away again. It would mean that it kept myself, Didier and Buchy out of the Corporals' radar, whom within a week of finishing on the Milan course had started messing us about. Normally it would be in the form of a snap inspection of our parade uniforms at 11 o'clock at night, which would always fail and would then be thrown out of the window onto the grass below. This meant having to wash and iron them before a second and third inspection or until the Corporal was happy. Not that he ever was, and his disapproval was normally accompanied by a smack in the mouth. Cowhead and another Corporal called Brunescu were the worst, but usually we got away with just a couple of inspections, unless of course they were drinking; in which case, we just kept on going until they'd demolished enough cases of beer to pass out.

We must have been like a trio of performing monkeys for them. A sort of welcome entertainment break that they could call upon whenever there was a lull in their conversation. Cowhead and Brunescu were the ringleaders and even Rocky had his moments. But what really annoyed me was that some of the rest of the platoon explained it all away as a sort of rite of passage.

Rubbish!

It was just an excuse for a couple of people with power to abuse that power, and then explain it away as somehow being an important part of the training process!

I probably would have had more respect for them if they had the guts to tell it how it was. But thankfully with the preparation for the commando school taking up most of our time we could just forget about it for the time being.

As it was, our preparation mainly consisted of getting beaten up anyway by the Adjutant, who was a qualified unarmed combat instructor. Just like the Chef back at Castel, he used the two-hour long training sessions as an opportunity to demonstrate his skill at being able to beat up a non-moving target that wouldn't fight back. Fortunately though, there was a sadistically marvellous moment during a demonstration of how to throttle someone with a short bootlace. Cowhead was the unwilling volunteer and after a few seconds of the oxygen being cut off from his brain, he collapsed unconscious only to come back round again a few moments later. Although none the worse for his ordeal, apparently, if he'd been throttled for any longer there would have been the possibility of brain damage. This I suspected was the Adjutant's reasoning behind picking Cowhead, as he acted like he was brain damaged most of the time anyway. The French call people like him: 'Gateau' and I suppose in one sense he made a great soldier. You could just wind him up, point him in the right direction, stand back and let him go. If you needed the bull in a china shop approach, then he was definitely your man.

As we passed over the drained moat of the Mount Louis fort, I could see ropes and cargo nets spanning the deep ravine which now served as some sort of an assault course, and I was glad that I'd never had a problem with heights. Some of the obstacles didn't look very pleasant at all and when we pulled up in the central courtyard, my initial enthusiasm started turning into apprehension.

The following morning we were introduced to our instructor who was one of the permanent teachers at the commando school. Our first lesson was unarmed combat, but fortunately for us he knew what he was doing and focused on teaching us exactly what we needed to know. We would start every day with an hour-long lesson, but would only focus on the basics of the different fighting styles, including judo and boxing as well as the French Army's own technique called 'corps a corps'. It was well taught and although taken very seriously was still great fun. It was also important to learn quickly, because part of the final tests would include defending ourselves against 15 attackers.

After lunch we spent a fascinating time learning how to tackle the different obstacles using the ingenious techniques that must have been perfected over the years. It was amazing how effectively you could shimmy up a drainpipe once you knew how. We were also taught how to climb up the inside of a large concrete pipe by starting off in a sort of sitting position on the floor and jamming yourself in by pushing outwards with your arms and legs. In this way you could slowly move upwards, and as long as you kept pushing outwards you shouldn't fall. Or at least that was the theory, which a few of the lads tried to disprove by slipping and landing with a thud. But the biggest motivation not to slip was due to the lack of a safety rope. The only protection we had was a counterweight on a pulley system. And not unsurprisingly, because it only weighed a couple of stone, falling was a pretty painful experience.

We also learnt how to abseil with all our gear and by the end of the first day I was having an absolutely fantastic time. It was just great fun learning all this new stuff and even the Corporals seemed a little more chilled out than usual. We even started having a laugh, much to the annoyance of the Adjutant who was taking the whole thing very seriously. And he blew his top a few days later when we were doing a covert river crossing in the dead of night.

The scenario was that we had to cross a fast-flowing deep river with only two lengths of rope, in complete silence. We'd been practising in daylight and as we lay up in all round defence one unfortunate Legionnaire had to make his way across the river using a makeshift flotation device, whilst towing a length of rope. Given that at night the air temperature dropped to below zero, it must have been absolutely freezing in the water. But once he was across we quickly set about setting up our rope bridge. This meant finding a tree on each bank and tying one rope like a tightrope and the other directly above it. This way you could walk on one of the ropes and the other, which should be just above head height, could be used to hold on to.

Everything was going well to begin with and I imagine the instructors must have been pretty impressed by our stealth. But they weren't counting on our secret weapon which came in the form of Legionnaire Dantes. Now in every Legion company there are a few people who work in the office doing the paperwork etc? And they are chosen for that job because they are probably better skilled with a notepad and pencil than they are with a rifle. Dantes was our office clerk and had been assigned to our platoon for the duration of the Commando school, and as he started out across the river everything seemed fine. When I'd made my own crossing I'd found it was a lot more difficult than I'd at first imagined. You needed to stay perfectly upright, but the rope was getting a little slacker each time someone crossed. Add to this the inconvenience of a rucksack, and you needed to concentrate hard not to loose your balance.

By the time Dantes reached the middle he started to get the wobbles and the more he tried to do something about it, the worse they became. It looked like something out of 'It's a Knockout' and he eventually fell forward so that the two ropes were more side by side than one above the other.

All that was needed was a pair a of stupidly big boots and a water cannon and I could imagine Stuart Hall and Eddie Wearing breaking down in fits of laughter as Dantes tried hard to flick himself back upright. But in doing so his momentum carried him over so he was now lying backwards. He kept on trying, and each time he over-shot, ending up either lying forwards or backwards.

The rest of us couldn't contain our laughter and the Adjutant called for silence, but because no one could be identified in the dark we just kept on. And it became even more comical when the Adjutant tried to shout quietly, but in doing so was becoming more and more irate.

His well oiled machine was being steadily humiliated by a pay clerk and a load of giggling Legionnaires. And he eventually lost the plot and told Dantes to drop into the river.

'I don't want to. It's going to be cold and I don't swim too good either'

Disobeying the Adjutant was never a good idea, especially not in front of other people from the French Army and the red mist must have descended. Pissed off, he stood up and shone his torch at Dantes, but that just set the instructors off on one.

'Put that torch out. It's supposed to be covert and you're behind enemy lines'

'SHUT UP! We're in France and I'm in charge here. Now get in that water Dantes you bastard before I drown you myself!'

It was hilarious to watch as Dantes slowly lowered himself into the river and made his way over to the river bank to be greeted with a welcome slap from the Adjutant. After a change a clothes though he was fine and was now well and truly one of the platoon.

Not that that actually stopped him over the next few weeks from showing us once again why he was better suited to his desk.

The course continued at an amazing pace and we would spend most days training hard and then putting into practice the day's teachings at night. All the time learning to do everything in complete darkness, and by the end of the first week we had already lost a few people to injury. I'd already gashed my head and badly split my hand open by having it rammed into a wall by a steel pole, but fortunately was still able to keep going. The injuries in the rest of the company though included a broken leg, a broken arm and one person who had been set on fire. Accidents were almost impossible to avoid in the dark and I was now just hoping that I'd make it to the end still in one piece. The assault courses for example were a nightmare to negotiate in the pitch black and freezing conditions. Weighed down by our rucksacks it was incredibly hard to try and climb up a steel drainpipe. It was like gripping a block of ice, which numbed your hands making the whole thing even harder. Given that you might have to shimmy up the equivalent of three storeys, falling was almost a given for a least a couple of people.

Dantes again though came to our rescue by managing to lift our spirits in a way that only he could.

During one of the night time assault courses that we were tackling as a team, he had been assigned to my group and about half way around we came to a 10 foot wall. Fino scaled it on his own and then disappeared over the other side. I slung his rucksack over the wall, followed by my own and went back to tell the rest of the group what we were up to.

Dantes was the first person I came to.

'Right... Make your way to the wall. Throw your rucksack over. Fino is waiting on the other side. Then climb over'

Ten minutes later we all re-grouped on the other side of the wall, ready to move to the next obstacle, only to discover that Dantes was missing his rucksack.

Moreau held his head in his hands, not really wanting to hear the answer as he asked Dantes where his rucksack was.

'I chucked it over that wall over there!'

'That's the wrong wall you knob head.... That's the outer wall of the fort. There's just a forest about a 100m below'

We all started laughing as Moreau stood motionless for a few moments, mulling the situation over and looking for a way out. He was a wily old fox as I'd seen the day before when during one of the assault courses, he pulled out a grappling hook he'd manufactured out of a standard issue metal water bottle, a rope and a piece of wood. It had enabled us to tackle one of the obstacles in super quick time, giving us one of the fastest times ever seen at the school and on inspection of our rucksacks, once taken apart, there was nothing that looked out of place.

After a moment's silence he asked for a couple of straps and a poncho, which he then made into a sort of rucksack. Not that convincing, but hopefully we'd get away with it.

'Okay. When we get to the end of the assault course.... Dantes....you stand in the centre of everyone whilst the instructor de-briefs us. It's going to be dark and hopefully he won't notice your rucksack is different'

'Yes Sergeant'

'Oh and Dantes....you'd better pray he doesn't notice. If I have to do this assault course again....I promise you....you're going to follow that rucksack!'

Amazingly we got away with it and the instructor even praised us for our agility at night. Half an hour later we were using those skills for real as Dantes sneaked past the guards and out of the fort in search of his rucksack, and was greeted by cheers when he arrived back undetected and holding his trophy.

After a week of training we left the fort and headed east towards the coast and the small harbour town of Collioure on the Mediterranean. Here we would again be put through our paces on the assault courses, but would also focus on explosives and large scale commando raids.

The assault courses here were more a test of your nerve and confidence, rather than your physical ability, as they normally required some delicate footwork hundreds of feet above crashing rocks. My least favourite was the cliff jump. This was simply a tree trunk shaped steel tube, slightly thinner than an oil drum, set vertically about four feet from the edge of the cliff face. All you had to do was jump from standing, and grip onto the pole. Trouble was....there's nothing to grip onto on a steel tube, so you had to jump upwards and outwards to hit the pole whilst still moving horizontally. If you just limply left the cliff face, you'd hit the pole already falling, making it almost impossible to grip onto. It was one of the most nerve-wracking things I'd ever done and whether or not it was the crashing waves below that added to the atmosphere, but more than one of us hesitated when given the order to go. I willed myself off the edge of the cliff, but somehow my feet were not connected to my brain and they stayed glued to the rock face. On the second order to jump though I managed to engage with them and leap as high as I could, gripping the tube like my life depended upon it. Sliding down afterwards onto a platform a hundred foot below was relatively easy by comparison and I was just glad to be back on solid ground.

The week at Collioure was great fun and culminated in a test that would require us to use all the skills we'd learnt so far. If we passed we would then once again make our way back to Mount Louis for the final week.

I would also highly recommend that if you ever find yourself in Collioure and fancy something a bit different from wandering around the usual tourist shops, then take a walk down the coastal footpath and look up at the old fort. You'll get a great view of the assault courses and may even see some Legionnaires launching themselves off the cliffs.

As for the final test though, it was designed to test the skills of the whole company, from the commander to the lowest ranking Legionnaire, as we mounted an assault from the sea on another fort a few kilometres down the coast.

Our team would be making the initial assault, scaling the cliff face and walls of the fort in darkness, before securing the outer perimeter so that the rest of the company could fly in by helicopter and lay the charges to destroy the radio communications. Once blown, we could all be extracted by the helicopters.

The spray kicked up by the fishing trawler was freezing as we stood on the outside of the rail waiting to make our leap into the blackness. With the lights on the boat out, I could clearly see the coast lit up like a Christmas tree and with the full moon reflecting off the water, visibility was good. This though made our approach all the more visible to the enemy, but at least once at the foot of the cliffs the light should hopefully make our climb a little easier.

I had a paddle in one hand and a waterproof bag in the other. The trawler started to slow down and we knew we were getting close to our drop-off point. Hopefully from the fort, a fishing trawler in the distance shouldn't create too much attention and as we made a pass, the skipper gave us the order to go. Our dingy went first and as I hit the sea, the sudden shock of the cold water caused me to gasp for breath. I concentrated hard on not letting go of anything and staying perfectly still until the wake caused by the trawler had settled down.

Clambering into the small inflatable dinghy we started paddling towards the cliffs, with Moreau directing us to a small inlet from where we could make our ascent. It was tough going but the freezing temperatures of our soaking uniforms only seemed to spur us on, and with our blackened up faces, we eventually arrived undetected at the base of the cliff and unloaded our climbing gear.

The 'attack on the fort' was a standard test for every unit that did the commando course, and so its occupants knew an attack was imminent. But most units made their assault overland and so hopefully our plan would take them completely by surprise.

It was Fino who made the initial climb, and making good progress we all followed him up to a ledge after he'd secured a rope. I knew that another assault group would be tackling the other cliff face and that timing was paramount if we were going to take out the two guard positions simultaneously. With my heart pounding, we eventually located ourselves just below the enemy position; still with half an hour to spare before the helicopters were due to arrive. Five minutes before that we would take out the guard position giving the main assault groups every opportunity to storm the fort. With everything going to plan and twenty minutes to wait in silence, I looked out across the sea from my vantage point and watched the night start to give way to day. But with the temperature still around zero I readjusted my woolly hat and blew onto my hands, trying to get some feeling back, when Moreau told us to get ready.

On his command I would launch two grenades into the enemy position and the rest of the team would open up with their FAMAS's.

The guard must still have been half asleep when the first grenade landed in his bunker followed a moment later by another. Within seconds of the grenades going off, which was followed by a hail of automatic fire, Moreau had scaled the last few metres of rock face and had the guard pinned to the floor by placing his knee in the small of his back. The sounds of explosions echoed around the fort as the other teams mounted their assaults and no sooner had we captured the first enemy position; we moved through and attacked a second. Green flares streaked into the sky signalling that we'd secured the outer wall of the fort and the main gate. Seconds later, a wave of helicopters came racing in low and fast along the coastline using the cliffs for cover and only exposing themselves at the very last moment before landing practically on top of the fort. Legionnaires poured out, sprinting through the main gate towards the communications centre, throwing grenades through open windows and shooting at anyone who ventured from the buildings. With the charges laid, there was a mass of shouting and commotion as teams briefly regrouped before leaving. I descended the outer walls into the main courtyard and along with Fino we followed the exodus of Legionnaires towards the waiting helicopters. A loud explosion was heard as we lifted off and our helicopter dropped almost vertically off the cliff face in order to pick up speed as we made good our escape, skimming only a few feet above the surface of the water.

It was a fantastic success and the instructors heaped praise on us for the ingenuity and speed of the attack. But this praise was unfortunately short-lived as the practicalities of soldiering took over. We still had another week to go and almost as soon as the raid was over we were packing our gear and loading up the trucks again for the journey back to Mount Louis.

A heavy snow had fallen during our week away but with the roads already cleared, apart from the cold it was an incredibly enjoyable and picturesque journey. The first snowfalls in any mountain range always look spectacular. And with the combination of bright sunshine and clear thin air I could see for miles. It was the freshness of the virgin snow on the peaks that looked so wonderful, but the guard on the main gate of Mount Louis didn't seem to share my thoughts, stamping his feet in the cold and just about managing a salute before returning to the warmth of his hut.

Three days later after more hand to hand combat training and learning how to make improvised mines from Tupperware boxes and shaped charges from champagne bottles, (not that a bottle of champagne is something that you would normally find just lying around….but then again I suppose this is France) we were ready for the final tests. The weather was bitterly cold when four of us paraded in the moat of the old fort for the unarmed combat test. There was a light snow falling and when Rocky's name was called out the rest of us were herded into a sort of large storeroom, which had been hollowed out of the outer wall, and the door was shut behind us.

We couldn't see anything of what was going on, but we could hear shouting from the instructor and although muffled it didn't sound pleasant. Twenty minutes later the door swung open and Rocky collapsed onto the floor. He was soaking wet, covered in mud and ice and unable to speak as he sucked in huge lungfuls of air. He looked a mess as he lay motionless on the freezing cold stone floor and my mind raced with what he'd been through!

'Bollocks to this. I'm going next'

Although we were only dressed in our thin combat fatigues, I quickly started undoing my jacket and taking my t-shirt off. It wasn't going to do me any favours in the next twenty minutes but at least I'd have something dry to put back on.

'NEXT!'

After being in the semi-dark of the storeroom, the brightness of the daylight took a few seconds to get used to and at first all I could make out was a huge figure coming towards me. It was an instructor I'd not seen before. He was a huge black guy and the only way I can describe him, is really hard looking, really pissed off looking and coming straight towards me.

In that split second before the storm though everything seemed calm and I just remember thinking 'Oh Shit….Ah well….Fuck you!'

For the next fifteen minutes there was a barrage of orders that were never ending and were designed to run me into the ground.

Roll forward! Roll backward! Sit down! Stand up! Faster! Faster! Pick that boulder up and sprint back here! Put it down! Pick it up! Faster! Put it down! Pick it up! Roll in that mud! Start doing push ups!

The mud was semi-frozen and my hands had gone numb as I started doing press-ups. His boot was on the back of my neck, pushing my face into the mud and making it impossible to breath and forcing me to use all of my strength just to do a single press-up. After only fifteen minutes of this type of madness it was virtually impossible to breathe and I was so knackered my lungs felt like they'd been burnt from the ice cold air. It was painful to breathe and my legs felt like jelly, which reminded me of watching boxers on the telly struggling to stand still.

I staggered to my feet and he punched me in the chest which sent me flying. But I was so completely exhausted I'd hadn't even seen it coming.

'Stand up! Come here!'

'Punch me!'

I barely had enough energy to stand up and I threw a punch towards his face. It was blocked easily and my feet kicked from under me which landed me on my back once again.

'Stand up! Follow me!'

We sprinted around the corner where there were fifteen guys dressed from head to toe in protective body armour. They formed a circle around me and I just tried to stand my ground.

I didn't even have enough energy for a pleasant conversation....let alone a fight!

'Protect Yourself!'

One by one they came, each with a pre-scripted attack. A head lock from behind, a punch to the face or a wooden knife into the guts. The training must have taken over at some point as I remembered the lessons and the different moves to defend myself. An arm block....A wrist lock....or an elbow to the face. Either way I managed to survive, but as I collapsed onto the floor of the storeroom I could see Rocky was still motionless.

Valera was next out, leaving behind a very pale looking Fino deep in contemplation. I couldn't even speak to answer his questions and just made a few meaningless hand gestures which was probably for the best. After a few minutes I started shivering as the cold floor sucked the warmth out of my body and I forced myself to take off my sodden jacket and put on my dry t-shirt. I don't know whether or not it helped, but at least I felt like I was doing something. And by the time Fino came staggering in like an old drunk that had been in a bar brawl, I was just about ready to move. The four of us made our way back to the barracks where Moreau greeted us with the good news that we'd be leaving in half an hour for the final set of tests. A two-day march through the hills that would take in river crossings, explosive tests and everything else we'd been taught over the last three weeks. We were also told to pack what we didn't need onto the trucks because we'd be going straight from the end of the march to Perpignan, where we'd hitch a ride back to Corsica aboard a Transal and parachute back into Calvi.

I'd never marched through the snow before and our lightweight summer sleeping bags were wholly inadequate for the job, ensuring we spent most of the night shivering. Fortunately though the Adjutant was in one of his more cunning moods and after completing the explosive tests, we set off in the direction of the next check point. The plan was to reach the next checkpoint, which was a hut in the mountains, where we'd find the written location of the final test. What the instructors didn't know was that the Adjutant had got one of the admin staff drunk, who'd then given away all the locations of the tests. As it was, we were only about 5km from the final test and had no desire to march 10km into the mountains trying to find a hut only to have to march another 10km to the test location.

So as it was, after getting a small fire going to dry ourselves out, we arrived at the final test fully refreshed and went straight into the assault course. Again putting in one of the fastest times they'd ever seen!

Maybe fate had the last laugh after all though when we parachuted back into Calvi. Unknown to us, Corsica was experiencing one of the warmest Novembers in history but we'd jumped still wearing thermal underwear, fleece jackets and Gortex waterproofs. With our rucksacks on our backs and carrying our parachutes, we sprinted to the forming up point in glorious sunshine, sweltering in the heat and arriving absolutely exhausted.

'Boarding the plane for our first jump'

'The assault course over the moat at Mont Louis'

'Myself and Ducs' at Brazzaville Airport'

'Human roadblock- the black dots on the
ground are all empty bullet cases'

'Nuns camped outside our camp'

'Our Toyota 4x4 – Machine Gun optional'

'Civilians being evacuated from The Congo– note
the cameraman getting his pictures'

'One last photo – just prior to leaving the airport'

'Government troops in Central Africa'

'Our medical clinic at the factory'

'Parachuting onto the sandbar'

'The five-hour assault course'

'Cookery lesson in the jungle!'

'On parade in Corsica'

New Arrivals

With five weeks to go before Christmas there was a lull in the training calendar and far from being something to look forward to, I'd discovered that as a new Legionnaire down time was never a good thing. In fact down time didn't really exist for new Legionnaires. Down time for the platoon meant that a new Legionnaire would work harder and be messed around doing pointless jobs whilst the Corporals sat around gobbing off. The evenings would then be spent cleaning something for the hundredth time whilst some semi pissed up tosser basked in the power that rank gave him. A favourite little job would be for a Corporal to take a bar of soap into the toilets and with the aide of a razor, stamp hundreds of small shavings of soap into the floor. It took hours cleaning them all up and ensured we'd be working most of the night.

This type of rubbish really got under my skin as it was just completely unnecessary. But I was fortunately rescued from this plight in an unexpected, but all the same very welcome way.

All jobs in the Legion are carried out by Legionnaires, whether they are cooks or admin clerks, and to supplement the demand for these jobs everyone has to train up with a second speciality. The choice is not great and is generally between either being a cook or a parachute packer....neither of which appealed. Working in the cook house a couple of days each month dishing out greasy food to a thousand hungry Legionnaires is not exactly what I had in mind when I'd joined. And neither was working on a production line packing parachutes. But unfortunately there was no getting away from it. It was only going to be for a few days each month, so maybe I was being precious, but I really didn't fancy it at all. I was trying to put it off as long as I could and so when the chance of learning the bugle came along I jumped at it. Not only would it mean I wouldn't have to train as a cook or parachute packer, it also meant that for the next month I'd be spending every day away from the platoon.

Fantastic!!

The bugle is played every day in the Legion: to march the guard on, raise the flag, announce meal times and at the end of the day, 'lights out'. It would mean that the bugler did a few more guard duties than most, but for me that was far more preferable than cooking up sausage butties.

The bugle or 'clairon' as the French call it was difficult to learn. It was longer than the normal stubby bugle used by the British and American army, giving more mellow and softer notes rather than sharp blasts. About the same length as a trumpet, it took patience and hours of practice to get a decent sound out of it. But after a month of practising all day every day, the hairs on the back of my neck stood up when I played 'The Last Post' in the final exam. Only two of us out of the six who'd started had completed the course, and although not the most military thing I'd done since joining, I was still extremely proud.

With the end of the course, Christmas was only a week away and the platoon had been working hard converting one of the rooms into a bar. It was traditional in the Legion that every platoon had its own bar that was open for the week between Christmas and New Year, and enormous effort was put into making it better than anyone else's. Not only for the prestige of having the best bar in the regiment; it was also an excellent way to swell the platoon's coffers. Money that would then be spent on buying us bits of kit the French Army didn't supply. We worked tirelessly knocking down walls, re-plastering and creating an African themed bar complete with a grass roof. Unfortunately though, once open, the Corporals took over and it just became a place most of the Legionnaires wanted to avoid. But with over thirty bars to choose from we were never short of a place to get a drink. My personal favourite was the Moroccan themed bar complete with huge cushions to chill out on and 'hubbly bubbly' pipes to puff on. It was a fantastic time and during the evening of Christmas Eve the whole regiment had an enormous party. There was an incredible amount of food that the kitchens had worked for days to prepare and cases of beer and wine stacked high. The food was of a superb standard and we filled our stomachs on traditional French dishes like cassule, duck patés and yes....snails. Every Legionnaire was given a present from the Company Commander and far from being some cheap tat, I got a good quality Casio sports watch and Leatherman penknife.

We then sang our Company and Regimental songs before performing our platoon 'sketches'. These were ten-minute stage performances written and performed by the Legionnaires and were our one chance to get our own back on the senior ranks. Ours was a parody of the overly complicated and bureaucratic way the French do things, added to the Legion mentality of only the Legionnaires actually doing any work. We brought the house down as we portrayed the lowest ranking Legionnaire doing absolutely everything and Sergeants refusing to lift a finger to help. Even during a staged attack, completely surrounded and about to be overrun they refused to move before the right forms had been filled in. And having poked fun at everyone we could think of, we moved back to the bars, where we drank until daylight before I finally fell asleep.

It was an incredibly traditional evening that hadn't changed in years and showed the importance with which the Legion still placed on its 'special days.' Everyone was expected to attend, even the senior ranks irrespective of whether they had their own family in town.

Christmas Day might be a time for their own family, but Christmas Eve was for their Legion family!

For the Legion, Christmas is more important then New Year and so 1997 was 'rung in' in a more subdued manner, with a few drinks in the barracks, and for me it was a time of reflection. It had been my first Christmas in the Legion and there were still four more to go before I'd finished my contract. In less than twelve months I'd completed basic training, the Parachute course, the Milan course, the Commando course and the bugle course. My feet

DIARY OF A LEGIONNAIRE

had hardly touched the ground and I'd learnt that that was not necessarily a bad thing for a new Legionnaire. I could only imagine what the coming year might hold, but rumours were already circulating that we'd be deploying to Africa in May.

Good news as that was, that still left five months of hard training ahead of us and it had been decided that we would be fitting in a major helicopter exercise, another trip to France for some live firing of the Milan, and a Regimental tactical march, as well as our own training in the platoon.

The New Year also brought some other good news in the form of three new additions to the platoon. Not only did this mean that Didier, Buchy and I were no longer the lowest of the low, but one of the new guys was English. Tom had served in the Coldstream Guards and after a couple of years in civvy street had joined the Legion. Originally from Birmingham I suppose he could best be described as a typical squaddie. He was a born cynic, cocky as hell, full of shit most of the time but one of the best soldiers I ever knew. There was also a Belgian lad who spoke English and a Russian who completed the trio.

The new intake was not just restricted to the Legionnaires. We also had a new Sergeant who would be taking over from Moreau, who would now stand in as the Sergeant Chef in the Platoon.

Alf was from Sweden and rumour had it that he'd held a senior position in a large multinational corporation. With access to company funds, he had decided to go on a spending spree with the company credit card. And after a holiday in Rio de Janeiro, complete with a new wardrobe of clothes, he'd decided to join the Legion and keep a low profile for a few years.

His name came from his unfortunate striking resemblance to a puppet character of the same name. It had been a popular American 'sit com' in the 1980's and Alf possessed the same rubbery features and huge nose.

He was a big guy and although he tried hard to act tough he was too decent a bloke to really carry it off. This place was so full of cruel bastards it had become all too easy to spot the good guys. After only a couple of days under his command it was obvious to all that although he might not be the most naturally gifted soldier, he made up for it in spirit. Whatever the job….he always gave 110%.

The first big test for Alf was the helicopter exercise and he was out to impress the Adjutant in any way he could. Whilst the rest of the platoon sat around watching, Valera, Rocky, Fino, Ducs, Jacques and I were going through the drill of how to get out of a helicopter for about the tenth time.

'OK! When I get the signal….Rocky….you open the door….I'll go first followed by everyone else….run for 50m….then go to ground! Got it! Right….lets go through it one more time'

I know he wanted to impress….but how hard is it to get out of a helicopter? It's not like it's the first time we'd ever done this type of thing.

Once we were actually airborne though and speeding through the mountains of Corsica it felt great. Our mission was to secure one of the flanks of an assault, and as we came in to land on the slope of a hill we prepared ourselves to exit. The tension mounted and we all readied ourselves to sprint as soon as the wheels touched the ground. Alf turned and gave the thumbs up to Rocky who automatically pulled back the side door on the chopper. With his rucksack over one shoulder, Alf turned to us and as if in some cheesy war movie shouted….'Follow me lads'….and disappeared out of the side door.

But no one followed Alf as the helicopter was still hovering at fifteen feet looking for the best place to land, and I could see Valera trying hard to control his laughter. But as the wheels touched the hillside and still wearing a huge grin, he looked at us and shouted…. 'Follow *me* lads'….and we sprinted up the hillside. Alf, who was still rolling around on the floor had fortunately landed in a bog that the helicopter had been trying to avoid; and apart for being covered in mud and having split his pants, exposing his bright white underpants, was none the worse for his fall. He joined us moments later as if nothing had happened.

Although nowhere near as competent as Moreau, Alf was a good bloke. And in this place….that went an awful long way!

Over the next couple of months time dragged, and although the days were packed with training and sport, there was little to occupy us in the evening. For the Corporals that meant participating in their favourite pastime of drinking and knocking hell out of the new guys. I lost count of the number of times that Tom and the new guys would appear for morning *appel* with black eyes or fat lips. It was depressing to see and there is nothing that is more frustrating than seeing a mate taking a beating and have to stand by completely helpless. Not that Tom couldn't take it.....he was tough lad. But there comes a point when people just decide they don't want to take it any more and leave. Great significance is placed on tradition in the Legion and whether they liked it or not, desertion is as big a tradition as anything else. It was difficult to escape with the Military Police patrolling the airports. But if you were determined enough, then you stood a good chance of getting away. Andre back at the 'Farm' had taught me that, and I couldn't see Tom hanging around much longer.

The Belgian lad had disappeared after only a month and the Russian had 'flipped' and walked into the guardhouse asking to be put in jail, claiming he'd rather spend the next five years locked up than one more day in the Milan Platoon.

I realised just how lucky I'd been having joined the platoon during the Milan course and then heading off to Mount Louis. It had meant that I'd been with the platoon nearly five months before settling into barrack life, and this had protected me from an awful lot of 'bullshit'. Tom though, was now the last man standing of his intake and I just hoped he'd decide to stay. But things came to a head a few weeks later one Saturday evening in the barracks. Back home, a usual Saturday night for Tom was a skinfull of beer and a fight, so being given the night off, he did what came naturally....and drank. Being called into the corridor by the Corporals a few hours later, he shook his head and opened the door. The beer had loosened his tongue though and without thinking he answered back to Corporals.

There was a moment's silence when everyone computed what had just been said and what was about to happen. The adrenaline must have kicked in and for Tom it was either fight or flight. With a case of beer on board a switch simply flicked in his brain and he instantly turned from a placid bloke having a drink to a psychopathic 'football hooligan'.

He just stood his ground, fronted them and screamed at the top of his voice in English.

'COME ON THEN....ALL OF YOU....RIGHT NOW....
COME ON....WHAT THE FUCK ARE YOU WAITING FOR?'

Cowhead moved half an inch and then thought better of it. He could probably have knocked Tom clean out. But Tom still had a beer bottle in his hand and Cowhead knew enough to know that going up against a pissed-up madman with a glass bottle, anything could happen. They had pushed Tom too hard over the last couple of months and only a week before had pinned him against the wall with a knife to his eye. Now the boot was on the other foot and Cowhead thought better of it. Rocky didn't move either, which was no real surprise, but just looked at Cowhead for guidance.

The shouting must have been heard by an Irish Sergeant from another platoon who'd been working down stairs and he broke the silence when he rounded the corner.

'You....Put that fucking bottle down now!....Get yourself downstairs and start scrubbing the floor!'

Tom realised this was his way out of the situation and instantly obeyed.

Turning to Rocky and Cowhead, the Sergeant told them to get back in their room.

'But Sergeant ....we take care of the discipline in THIS platoon'

'Did you just answer me back?'

'No Sergeant'

'Good....Now FUCK OFF!'

The sergeant had played the situation superbly and about as well as it was possible to do. Just because some of the Corporals and Sergeants believed in banging heads together, it didn't mean that everyone did. The trouble was that outside of your own direct chain or command, it was difficult to say, or do anything about it. Simply stopping the Corporals wouldn't have done Tom any favours anyway. In fact it probably would have made life worse for him if it looked liked he needed someone to step in and help him out. The Sergeant knew damn well what had been going on, but by punishing Tom it didn't look like he was trying to stop anyone being bullied. It had simply looked like he was stopping a fight taking place. He had though prevented Tom from getting a very nasty kicking. He knew it....we knew it....and Tom certainly knew it.

Not that this little setback deterred Cowhead and the others. Within a couple of days things were back to normal, with our evenings being spent at 'their disposal.' But now it was not just the new guys but all of the Legionnaires, including those with two or three years of service. But there was a problem with this. Just as brutal discipline was 'tradition' in the Legion, so was length of service. In fact length of service was almost as important as rank. It's difficult to explain how important length of service is. But it commanded instant respect and by messing with the older Legionnaires, they were messing with tradition. And tradition after all is what kept the status quo in the Legion. You couldn't ignore it without consequences. This then, could only last so long and one evening, as we lined up in the corridor at the request of Brunescu, he suddenly punched Rustick in the face. The thing with Rustick is that he was one of the senior Legionnaires and should have been past all of this type of messing around. Although a quiet bloke who kept himself to himself, he had also boxed at a national level back home in Poland as a light middleweight. Punching him under any circumstances would be regarded as fairly mad. But in front of junior Legionnaires from his own platoon, it was just completely crazy.

But Rather than punch him back, he astonished us all by just grabbing Brunescu's arms and telling him to 'Take it easy!'

Brunescu responded by lowering his fists, almost acknowledging his mistake. And as he did, Rustick punched him. Only once just below the eye, but that was all it took. I'd seen a lot of fights in this place and been involved in a few, but they were probably best described as 'scraps.' Watching someone who new what they were doing though was just on another level. The punch came from nowhere and was the most powerful and accurate I'd ever seen. But amazingly, Brunescu was still standing. I couldn't believe that it would have been possible, as he rebounded off the wall and stood perfectly still. But his brain must have already switched off and we watched mesmerised as his eyes rolled back and a second later his knees buckled and he crumpled like a concertina. No one moved to help and after a few moments of unconsciousness he started trying to drag himself along the floor. But being one of the guys who'd been giving us a hard time for the last couple of months, no one felt inclined to help him out. Violence is always a horrible sight, but at the same time I just couldn't muster any sympathy for him. He was a bully and as I watched him pathetically trying to drag himself towards his room, still unable to stand, I was glad.

Rocky came out of his room with a fag hanging out of his mouth wandering what was going on. But he only got two words into his sentence before Rustick flicked out a jab which caught him in the mouth and knocked him off his feet.

For a moment there was a sensation that anything might happen and thoughts of facing up to all of the Corporals passed down the line. The moment was lost though when Valera popped his head out of his room and ordered everyone back into their rooms with a sort of, 'the party's over' type speech. A Legionnaire punching a Corporal was one thing, but disobeying them en masse was quite another and we retreated back into our rooms and settled for a draw.

Rusktick's attack could not go unpunished and a day later he was paid a visit by the Corporals. Letting it go would have undermined their authority but at the same time everyone liked Rustick. Even the decent Corporals like Valera and Jim understood the importance of maintaining the rule of command, and fortunately Rustick did the honourable thing and took his beating without complaint. They went as easy on him as they could and in so doing the natural order was restored.

But any hope that things would now at last quieten down were short-lived and within a week normal order of play had resumed.

But it couldn't last much longer as things were now getting to breaking point. Not only had we lost two of the new guys, one of the other Legionnaires had a burst ear drum and was now in hospital. At this rate there wouldn't be any Legionnaires left to order about. If we could just get rid of Cowhead and Brunescu then things would change. But that was never going to happen and so things seemed set to continue.

After yet another evening of mindless work into the early hours, Fino and I came back to our room where Valera was lying on his bed reading a Spanish newspaper, by the light of his bedside lamp.

Cowhead came bursting in to the room and put the main light on screaming something unintelligible at us in his usual manner. Pissed off at having his relaxing read interrupted Valera looked up.

'Oy....put the light out'

'Yeah sorry Valera....I'll only be a minute....I just wanted a word with these two'

'I don't want it out in a minute....my room....I want it out now'

'Okay....I'll only be a minute'

'No....put the fuckin' light out - Now!'

'All right....take it easy....'

Valera got up, walked over towards Cowhead and put the light out before returning to his bed.

Putting the light back on Cowhead looked almost puzzled....' Fuckin' hell....what's your problem?'

Again Valera got up, walked over to the light switch and then to my amazement, head-butted Cowhead in the face, knocking him into the corridor.

I couldn't believe what I'd seen. Valera was no match for Cowhead, who after a few seconds recovering from a blow that would have finished most people off, came straight back at Valera and almost picked him off the floor, grabbing him by the throat and slamming him into the wall. I must have had the 'rabbit caught in the headlights' look about me and was stood open mouthed as Cowhead pulled back his fist. Valera might not have been a great fighter, but obviously knew a lot more than I'd given him credit for.

Because he reached forward and after taking a good firm grip on Cowhead's bollocks pulled and squeezed as hard as he could.

Now there is an instinctive male reaction whenever you see this type of thing happening, and Fino and I looked at each other with that look on our faces as if we'd just bitten on something slightly sour. It was a telepathic moment when everyone was thinking the same thing.

God….I bet that really hurt!

But before he'd made a conscious decision as to what to do next, Cowhead's body instantly submitted and he started pleading to be let go. Valera relaxed his grasp, but only after another squeeze, and left him lying in the corridor nursing his swollen balls.

This place seemed to get madder by the second and Valera casually walked back into the room, switched off the main light and continued reading his newspaper. I was stunned and honestly think he'd purposely picked a fight with Cowhead to stick up for us. It might sound a little strange but it was obvious he didn't agree with messing us around. As a junior Corporal though there was not a lot he could do about it. I'd always found that seeing people bullied had been an incredibly frustrating experience. Not being able to do anything had been horrible and there was no reason to think that it was any less frustrating for Valera. So given the opportunity of getting rid of some of that frustration, there was no way he was going to hold back. There had been real venom in his attack. You could see it in his eyes. He had wanted to really hurt Cowhead and whether or not I was right, one thing was definite. It wasn't just over a light switch.

The platoon was now split into two camps. Legionnaires on one side, Corporals on the other, with a few people like Valera and Jim sat in the middle. It seemed completely insane that we should be fighting amongst ourselves instead of developing as a platoon. The last few months had strengthened the bond between the Legionnaires though, brought together by our collective suffering. In many ways it felt like basic training again, except there was now no light at the end of the tunnel. No finishing line to cross. No counting down of the days until the end. This was just how it was and it didn't seem to be about to change any time soon. But we weren't raw recruits any more either and with a tour of Gabon now definitely on the cards, talk began of putting an end to things.

Gabon's capital city of Libreville was apparently no different from many West African cities and could be an extremely dangerous place to be. During the platoon's previous tour, one of the Legionnaires had been shot on a night out and another had been attacked with a machete. And this got many of the lads plotting against Cowhead. Because even a half serious injury would send him back to France!

I think like most of the Legionnaires, I didn't feel comfortable with plotting to put a Corporal in hospital. But neither could we continue to let someone abuse his power in the way he had for the next couple of years, or for however long in took to get promoted ourselves. It's not like we could go to the Adjutant. For one thing we couldn't go crying, and for another, he was the one who wanted the platoon run like this. And so it might not be the best plan in the world, but for the time being, it was the only one we had!

Our plan was set and for the next couple of weeks we settled down to accepting the rule of law within the platoon. With Gabon only a month away things no longer seemed so bad. But it was Cowhead, drunk on his own power who eventually bit off more than he could chew. It was gone one o'clock in the morning and after hours of messing around he ordered us to parade in the corridor with our rucksacks and helmets. Tired and pushed to the end of our tether, we snapped. With an order to do press-ups, no one moved. We took off our helmets and stood our ground. No one had decided that this was to be the moment. It just happened. Whatever the future held it couldn't be any worse than this. We numbered twenty and each had a steel helmet in our hand, and I suppose in military terms we out-gunned and outnumbered them. If we were ever going to make an impact it had to be now. Cowhead, slow in grasping the situation punched one of the lads in the stomach and reissued his orders. We flinched en masse and he backed off a little, trying to figure out what to do next. In his world, he said and we did. It never got any more complicated than that.

And you could see his bewilderment as he tried to think of the right thing to say. Cowhead was no coward, he wasn't scared of us. He just hadn't been bright enough to read the situation before it got out of hand. But he could see we'd made our minds up and we weren't going to perform any more. And he pathetically reissued his order, but again no one moved. I could feel the tension and it was only going to take one person to twitch and we would have all pilled in on him. What could they do? Put us all in jail. So what! At least Cowhead would be out of the picture!

Cowhead's raised voice had drawn some attention and I saw Rocky's door move slightly before shutting again. But it was Rustick who broke the silence by simply stating that we were going to bed and wouldn't be out again if ordered to. To my amazement Cowhead seemed to accept this and let us go. No objection, no fight! Nothing! He just let us go! But what else could he do? Get pounded into next week and at the same time lose the respect of the other Corporals as someone who couldn't control the Legionnaires? Without the other Corporals coming out to stand with him he'd been left no choice.

The next morning there was a strained atmosphere in the platoon as we paraded for our normal Monday morning run. With no one mentioning the night's events, I wasn't sure whether Cowhead had said anything but I couldn't see what he could have gained by running to the Sergeants. Just as we couldn't complain about him, he would have been ridiculed for complaining about us. Besides, the Legion doesn't do subtle. If he had complained.....we'd have known about it by now.

As he often did, it was the Adjutant who led the run and at first everything seemed normal. We ran out of the back gate and headed up into the hills. The temperature was warm and with a steady pace it was quite a pleasant run. It was only after about ten kilometres that we realised our route was going to be a little longer than usual. He then dropped the bombshell that we'd be running 35km. That's about 22 miles!

Now I've never run a marathon. But if I did, I guess I'd be filling up on liquids before hand and drinking on the way around. I don't think I'd be having a croissant and a small cup of coffee for breakfast. Most people just looked at each other, rolled their eyes and shook their heads. The regimental march was only a couple of days away and it seemed that our preparation was to run a marathon through the mountains on no food.

Was this our punishment?

I don't know! Maybe it was just a coincidence. The Adjutant did have a habit of suddenly pulling stunts on us for no apparent reason. A couple of weeks beforehand we'd been out on manoeuvres in the jeeps when he suddenly stopped by the side of the road and ordered everyone out. We then lay on the tarmac and did 500 sit-ups before continuing on our way. He was definitely 'not all there' and even off duty it was obvious he needed help. He used to dress like Marlon Brando from the *The Wild Bunch*, complete with black biker's jacket, white t-shirt and cowboy boots. Driving around Calvi in his 1960's Ford Mustang Convertible with Chuck Berry blasting out of the stereo, the image was topped off with a cigarette that was permanently hanging out of his mouth at just the right angle to complete the 'rebel without a cause' look.

Maybe that's what happened if you stayed here too long. But given his track record, suddenly announcing the 35km run should not have been any great surprise.

The second hour of the run was hard going as we plodded up and down the hilly terrain. We ran down tracks, crossed streams and fought our way through the dreaded Maquis which clung to any part of our bodies that touched it, leaving its sticky resin as a reminder. Its distinctive sweet smell filled my nostrils and I started to regret not having had a decent drink before leaving. The platoon was already stretched out and seeing Cowhead in the rear brought a smile to my face. At least the great oaf was suffering more than most.

At last we stopped by a stream and drank the ice cold mountain water that burnt the backs of our throats, but had never tasted so good. And being near the front of the group had paid off because as soon as the tail-enders caught up we were off again, galloping up the road towards the horizon, three or four hundred metres above us.

It was a slow steady climb that seemed to take forever, and as we crested the peak in the road I could see a large valley stretching out towards the coast and the small town of Galeria in the far distance. The road could be clearly seen idling gently down the valley side for miles and unless we took one of the mountain tracks, it should be all downhill from now on. But after another hour of running my knees and ankles were in agony and I started to wonder if the run would ever end. We were miles from the camp and at a rough guess it would take us another two hours at least to get back. I looked behind and could see a trail of Legionnaires back up the mountain. I was knackered and couldn't believe he'd pulled a stunt like this. With little or no fluids on board most of us were suffering and were utterly pissed off. With the regimental march only a couple of days away I couldn't think of a worse preparation. But as we rounded a bend in the road we saw Moreau waiting with a truck loaded with water.

It was just like an oasis in the dessert. That sense of utter relief knowing the sensation of thirst is going to end, because dehydration is a horrible feeling. You can feel it happening as your body starts screaming at you for water. There is a sense of panic that something terrible is going to happen to your body if you don't drink something soon. Your head starts pounding and the smallest things begin to really annoy you.

And I couldn't see the point of running the platoon into the ground like this. It was just shear stupidity!

It was midday by the time the truck pulled back through the main gates and whether or not the run had been a punishment for the previous night I didn't know. But one thing was for sure. Corporal or Legionnaire….we all hated the Adjutant that day!

A couple of days later and still not feeling 100%, we boarded the Transal for the short flight to Bastia where we would be parachuting onto a Drop Zone south of the airport for the start of the march. The whole regiment would be jumping in stages and then tactically marching back to Calvi. The infantry companies would be marching in the valley floors where possible and we would be taking to the higher ground along with the mortar platoon. The height would enable us to provide fire support for the infantry companies, with the clear lines of fire that were necessary for our Milan anti-tank weapons.

The march was going to take three days and we'd cover at least 100km. Even the older Legionnaires were moaning that it was going to be a killer, and loaded down with the firing post I was just hoping I'd be able to keep up. I knew that marching with the infantry platoons was going to be tougher than usual. Not being laden down with heavy bits of kit, they could cover the ground quicker and wouldn't appreciate having to wait for us. I'd packed as much water as possible and was having a quiet moment to myself, when word passed down the line that the winds where too strong to jump and we'd be landing at the airport.

The news was met with quiet relief by most people. It wasn't that we didn't want to jump, but parachuting at night was precarious at the best of times and no one wanted to pick up a sprained ankle before the march. A slight twist might seem like nothing at first, but with our heavy packs and 100km of the Corsican mountains to cross it was better not to take the chance. Besides, if you did twist your ankle on the jump and mentioned it you'd be in the shit for trying to get out of the march. But if you said nothing and soldiered on until it became unbearable, you'd be in the shit for not having said something earlier!

The only downside was that the airport was 10km further away. But as ever in the Legion, just as you were starting to feel sorry for yourself you always came across someone worse off. Lydman was from Finland and had recently joined the mortar platoon. As he clambered off the plane I thought it must have been some kind of joke and couldn't help but start to giggle. He was wearing two heavily loaded rucksacks. One on his back and the other on his front with his head squashed somewhere in the middle. Because the rucksack came above head height, he couldn't see where he was going and would be spending the next three days staring at the back of the rucksack....four inches in front of his face!

He looked comical and Tom couldn't hold back from saying something.

'Hey Lydman....you off on your hols or something....I know you're new but didn't anyone tell you....it's one bag only mate!'

'Oh fuck off....fucking corporal told me I've got to carry his rucksack because he's got the base plate for the mortar'

Seeing poor Lydman with his two rucksacks made me feel almost lucky. The Milan plus my rucksack was probably of a similar weight but was much easier to carry. Even so, Lydman seemed in good spirits as we all set off into the night, towards the blackness off the mountains that encircled Bastia.

The night air was cool but within minutes I was sweating as we fought our way up the mountain paths. The Milan was already digging into my back and it felt like I was giving someone a fireman's lift up the side of a steep mountain pass. You only ever had one hand free and even though the full moon provided good light, scrambling up the mountain was tough work. Although no one spoke, there was the constant grunt of someone or other pulling themselves over a rock or forcing their way through the Maquis. The march had been predicted to take until 2 o'clock in the morning, but as with many military plans, timings go out of the window when the troops get on the ground. By 3 o'clock we were only halfway up the side of the mountain and looking back I could still make out the airport and the main road into Bastia. Distance wise we'd hardly moved and I was already knackered. Having set off at 7 in the evening we'd been marching uphill for over 8 hours, stopping every 2 hours for a ten-minute break. It was obvious the rest of the platoon was just as knackered and although no one had dropped off the pace, the high spirits at the start had long since disappeared. During the first couple of breaks, most people had taken their rucksacks off and moved around, making their uniform more comfortable or just chatting. Now most of us just slumped to the ground the moment we stopped and tried to sleep for a few minutes before the order came to move off.

Ducs was in front of me with the other Milan and I could see that he was struggling under the weight. I'd initially thought that carrying a missile would have been easier but given the thickness of the Maquis, the missile carriers spent much of their time dragging themselves through the hedges. Our beloved team leader Alf, although only carrying his own gear was already walking like he was on hot coals. I'd noticed he'd bought a pair of brand new boots, identical to the standard issue ones, but made of softer leather and a lightweight sole. I had a pair myself and they were incredibly comfortable to run in, but were horrible for marching long distance. It was like wearing a pair of flip flops and the unforgiving Corsican hills made them agonising for your feet. I'd made the mistake of wearing them on a much shorter march, but within a few hours I could feel every little stone pressing into the soles of my feet, giving the feeling of walking over a bed of hot coal. Alf still had two more days to go and the downhill bits would be even more painful. If I hadn't been feeling so knackered myself I would have felt sorry for him. But as it was, watching him walk around like his feet were on fire, grimacing with every step, looked hilarious and our entire group had to try hard not to laugh out loud. Just as with Lydman, right at the time you start to feel sorry for yourself you always see some poor sod worse off.

By 7 o'clock in the morning the light was up and although we'd crested the first peak we were still some distance from our lie up point. With the French Air Force using helicopters to act as an enemy reconnaissance force we couldn't afford to be caught out in daylight. The infantry companies would already be in place and so we had to get to our position as soon as possible. With no alternative the pace was increased and we eventually reached our destination just after 8 o'clock. We set the Milans overlooking the valley before finally collapsing, thoroughly exhausted. We'd been marching for just over thirteen hours, weighed down with heavy packs and I was completely dead on my feet. I wasn't sure how far we'd covered, but we still had two more days to go. We could only rest and eat for the next 9 hours before we'd be off again. I shovelled some food down and drank about a litre of sweet tea, and tried to sleep for a few hours before my watch on the Milan.

The second night probably wasn't as gruelling as the first, but felt just as bad. We weren't starting from fresh and the mountains seemed never-ending. As soon as we'd passed over one peak and descended down the other side, another appeared in its place and we were off again. Up and down we went most of the night until we'd slogged our way up the side of a mountain that took us six hours to scale. We set up camp just before daybreak and again tried to take as much food on board as possible. I was permanently thirsty and although I still had water left, Fino and a few others were getting low.

Before the march, I'd wandered how much water to take and initially had erred on the side of 'the lighter my pack the better.' But it had been Valera who had told me to take as much as possible. If I became hacked off with the weight.....I could always drink it. That kind of logic made sense to me and I was glad I'd listened to it. I also knew that Fino was too proud to ask for a drink, but was also too thirsty to refuse if I offered.

Utterly shattered, we shared a mug of coffee and laughed at Alf as he tiptoed past our bivouac. The 'hot coal' walk had since developed into a sort of breakdance routine which now involved his arms flaying around with every step.

En Afrique

The dense humid West African air hit me like a brick wall as I walked onto the runway. The palms of my hands started to sweat and I became out of breath just picking up my bags. The four-month tour of Gabon was a fairly standard tour for the Legion, after the French Government had retained a foothold in its former colony, but I was looking forward to it all the same. We had left the Milans back in Calvi and had now reverted back to being an infantry platoon for the duration of the tour. And although our team had stayed the same, we'd spent the last month training in our new roles. I was now the team sniper, carrying a 7.62mm bolt-action rifle with telescopic sight, and Ducs carried the Minimi. This was a belt-fed 5.56mm machine gun that could also take 30 round M16 magazines and was now standard issue in the regiment. Each platoon had three of the 'para' version of these which had a collapsible shoulder stock and shortened barrel. And with their high rate of fire they made an excellent addition to the platoon.

The 'Camerone' celebrations had also been fitted in before we left and they had made a welcome break to the training. Camerone takes place on the 30th April every year and commemorates the Legion's most famous battle, when in 1863 a company of sixty-two Legionnaires made a stand against an enemy force numbering over a thousand strong. Stranded in an old farmhouse, the Legionnaires, led by Captain Danjou repulsed wave after wave of enemy attack all through the day. Towards late afternoon, with Danjou already dead, the Mexicans finally penetrated the upper storey of the farmhouse, leaving the remaining Legionnaires to sprint across the courtyard and take cover in an outbuilding. Refusing an offer to surrender, the last six Legionnaires fixed bayonets, broke out of their position and charged the Mexican infantry.

Miraculously three Legionnaires managed to survive the charge and were allowed to live. Danjou's false wooden hand was picked up after the battle and still has pride of place in the Legion's museum in Aubagne. And it had been in front of this piece of history that I had taken the oath of allegiance when I'd joined.

Every year since, each regiment in the Legion celebrates this date with public parades and special events. The regiments also open their doors to the public who are free to wander around certain parts of the barracks. There're hot dog stands, beer tents and other stalls set up, with most platoons putting something on. We'd rigged up the Milan simulator for anyone who wanted to have a go, but there was also pistol shooting, rope slides and other carnival type stuff. It was also a relaxing time for us as well and apart from doing a few shifts on the stall, our time was free.

The party continued well into the night and although most of it is now a blur, I do remember walking down the corridor through a haze of green smoke after one of the mortar platoon had thrown a smoke grenade, and opening the toilet door only to come face to face with a donkey. The fact that it was wearing socks over its hooves and drinking out of the toilet might under different circumstances have seemed out of place. But here....it just blended into the madness!

The journey from the airport through the outskirts of Liberville was one of lush green grasses and corrugated shacks. The air was thick, and even with a breeze provided by the open topped truck the early evening temperature was unpleasantly sticky. Our barracks though were well designed with high ceilings and open doors at each end which created a natural flow of air. Our days started at 6.30 to escape the high afternoon temperatures, and within a couple of days we'd already started to acclimatise. During the next four months we'd be spending much of our time in the forest learning the skills of jungle warfare which was something I was really looking forward to. After all, this was the sort of thing I'd joined the Legion for in the first place. A day later though our plans were scrapped when we were unexpectedly put on twelve hours' notice to move.

The Congo, which neighbours Gabon's southern border, was becoming unstable after a successful military coup in neighbouring Zaire. The whole area is rich in mineral reserves and years of corruption and unrest had turned them into a tinder box for military takeovers. The Congo's wealth lay in its oil reserves which were being extracted with the help of French Oil Companies, whose workforce, many of them French civilians, lived in the capital city of Brazzaville. The army had started to splinter into separate groups, each with their own agenda and the government was desperately trying to re-establish control. Although they still had control of the capital, they were starting to lose command of the provinces and if the situation continued to worsen the French Government would take the decision to evacuate their civilians. It would be our job to seize control of the airport and establish a base on the outskirts of the capital, where we could co-ordinate their safe passage out of the country.

With no idea of when this order might come and with little information as to what awaited us on the ground, the barracks became a frantic hive of activity, from organising the big bits of kit right down to the mundane stuff like making sure we had enough pairs of socks. Not knowing how long we would be there or when we'd be re-supplied, we erred on the side of caution and loaded up with as much as we could carry. It's true that in every army during peacetime, store men guard their meagre supplies like a lioness protecting her cubs. And the Legion was no different, but as soon the operation was announced the key to the secret store was found and we soon became overloaded with extra bits of this and spare parts for that. I even ended up with pocketfuls of batteries for my night scope. If nothing else, at least I knew my walkman wouldn't be running out!

With no vehicles, we could only take what we could carry and by the time we'd finished packing we'd be having trouble walking off the back of the Transal, let alone fighting our way out! But with our gear ready it now just became a waiting game as our initial activity settled down into one of boredom. The situation in the Congo seemed to improve and our talk turned to standing down.

But a day later with the Congolese government losing parts of the capital city to the rebels a decision was taken. We'd be going in whilst the airport was still in government hands and we could secure a supply route into the country. Waiting any longer would mean having to re-capture the airport from an enemy force that was armed with artillery and light tanks. A tall order for anyone, but potential suicide for 200 lightly armed paratroopers.

With the job back on we loaded onto the trucks and headed towards the airport where the Transal was waiting in the fading light to fly us the 500 miles to Brazzaville. There was a strange atmosphere on board, of excitement and anticipation mixed with an apprehension of going into the unknown. A sudden realisation that this was now very real indeed. I'd initially joined the Legion hoping for adventure. I'm not sure that adventure was now the right word, but as the wheels left the ground I just hoped we would all be back to talk about it.

In true military style most of our ammunition had to be flown directly from France and was due to arrive in the Congo at the same time as we did. This meant that our initial assault was going to have to be one of the biggest bluffs in history. We were tasked with having to take over control of the airport from the government forces, but given the fluidity of the situation there was no guarantee that this would be straightforward. With rebel forces moving on the airport we couldn't wait any longer in Gabon and so we'd set off with no more than a handful of ammunition between us. I had a single round for the rifle and the rest of the platoon had no more than a few rounds each for their FAMAS's. Duc's Minimi, although being the same calibre as the FAMAS, took a different bullet and so he was formidably armed with no more than harsh language.

On the flight in, the company commander was sitting a few feet away from me and I watched as he stared at the floor deep in contemplation. He had a huge responsibility and if ever he needed to put on his poker face....now was the time. He was generally well respected by the Legionnaires, something that couldn't always be said about a lot of the other Legion Officers I'd met. He had previously been in command of the Regiment's Pathfinder platoon, who were the closest thing to Special Forces the Legion had. They used the latest free fall parachutes and were trained in close observation techniques and missions behind enemy lines. 'Le Capitaine' looked like he had the weight of the world on his shoulders, but he also possessed that natural French aloofness and I was certain that he could pull it off. Besides, he didn't really have any choice....there was no Plan B.

We hung onto the seats as the Transal felt like it was going into a vertical dive on its approach to the airport. The pilot must have than been hanging off the joystick as he levelled the plane off only seconds before I felt the wheels touch the ground, and the brakes screeched us to a sharp halt. The tailgate dropped and we deployed as quickly as possible. This was our most vulnerable moment, grouped together in a steel tube and surrounded by aviation fuel. A lucky RPG round from the fence could cause untold carnage, so we fanned out in all around defence. My night scope was working well and the blackness of night turned into a slimly green world. I could make out the perimeter fence and the thick jungle vegetation beyond. Surprisingly, there didn't seem to be any Congolese troops and given that rebel forces supposedly controlled the surrounding country side, the airport didn't seem to be very well defended at all.

We stayed in position as a second and third wave of Transals flew in until all 200 Legionnaires were on the ground. The airport takeover had seemed to come off without a hitch with the government forces handing over control. Our bluff had worked and given that government forces today could be rebel forces tomorrow, there was significant relief it had gone well. I could see our ammunition being loaded directly from one of the planes into small trucks and like everyone else I would feel a lot happier once we had something to defend ourselves with. The plan was now to leave a small force to protect the airport whilst the rest of us moved into a defendable location on the edge of town. This meant travelling through rebel held territory and unfortunately we'd only managed to commandeer two small trucks and so couldn't travel in force, but instead would have to go in waves.

The good news was that the Pathfinder platoon had secured our base camp and most of our troops had already made the journey and were in place. The bad news was that we would be the last to go using the same route as everyone else. Oh, and the real kick in the nuts was that some bright spark had loaded all our ammunition onto the trucks which had already left! This was now getting beyond funny and everyone started gobbing off as we climbed into the small trucks. Alf responded by barking out a few orders.

'You two can get in last....And make sure people can see you.'

'I've only got one round.'

'I've haven't got *any* fucking rounds.'

'Yeah well....you've got a big gun....that should scare a few people off.'

Ducs was still moaning as he pulled the shoulder stock out on the Minimi to increase its length and slapped an empty M16 magazine into the side. I hung the sniper rifle out over the tailgate in full view and hoped that our second bluff of the night would go as well as the first.

A coach that was now acting as an improvised gate was moved forward and we drove out of the airport and into the night. The tarmac road was not lit and I could clearly make out Brazzaville itself. We raced down one of the main boulevards and seemed to be the only people around. It was like being in one of those sci-fi films where someone has woken up after being in a coma and finds everywhere deserted. There was the odd vehicle that looked like it had been abandoned in a hurry but mostly there was just silence. The street lighting was dim, which only added to the eeriness of the place and made me feel even more vulnerable. Coming to a halt at some crossroads whilst the driver and Alf quickly checked the map, Ducs tapped me on the shoulder and pointed at something lying on the pavement a few metres away. A dead man's body lay bloated and bloodied on the ground. The pavement was dark with his blood and there was a small trail where he'd managed to crawl a few yards before dying.

'AK47'

Ducs had noticed their distinctive stubby 7.62mm bullet cases that littered the ground and indicated the method of execution. This guy was dressed in civilian clothing and his grey hair gave away his age. If this is what happened if you got caught on your own at night, no wonder the streets were empty. We continued towards our base camp and arrived to a frenzy of activity. We located the rest of the platoon and after grabbing a handful of rounds, once again set up a defensive line.

Daylight revealed that our base was located in the jungle on the edge of a minor road. There were a few dilapidated old concrete buildings dotted around the place giving the impression that at one time it had been an institution of some kind. But the jungle had long since reclaimed its territory making it difficult to identify what had really been here before. Our basic defensive perimeter was circular with each platoon having the responsibility of defending a small sector. There was also a rotating guard that secured the main gate and would act as a rapid deployment force. We immediately set about digging defensive positions along our sector that we could deploy too, and thirty metres behind these started clearing the jungle floor. This would be our living area and due to the thickness of the jungle, couldn't be seen from the outside. Here at least, we would be able to relax and sleep a little.

A decision had still not been made as to whether the French civilians were to be evacuated or not and so we made the most of this spare time by trying to build ourselves a home in the jungle.

The ammunition situation had improved significantly and I was relieved to be issued sixty rounds for the sniper rifle. Ducs' mood also improved considerably after he got his hands on 800 rounds for the Minimi and those with FAMAS's received 200 rounds each, two hand grenades and two rockets. These were small anti-tank rockets that were slid over the barrel of the FAMAS and fired directly at the target. Anti-tank was probably not the best description, but the 51mm shaped charge would certainly stop most vehicles.

A new problem also arose in the form of our lack of vehicles. If the order did come to evacuate the civilians we didn't have any means of doing so. There were reports that armoured vehicles were on the way from France, but no word on how long they would take to arrive, so a decision was taken to commandeer civilian vehicles.

Those people who had already decided to leave the country had been told to leave the keys to their cars in the ignition. Thus the airport car park was full of cars that might just suit our purpose.

Alf gave a simple order to come back with anything appropriate and we set off like a group of kids with the keys to the amusement park. There was a huge selection of expensive 4x4's and executive cars just waiting to be taken. Within minutes Ducs and Fino were donuting a 5 series BMW around the car park like they were Starsky and Hutch. I'd opted for luxury over practicality with a Lexus 4 wheel drive. But after an hour of fun and inappropriate choices, we had to settle for a couple of pickups and a 4x4. Spare flak jackets were slung over the sides of the pickups to offer minimal protection and the Minimi was then strapped to the cabin, so that a gunner could ride shotgun. Until the armoured personnel carriers arrived from France, putting one of these vehicles at the front and rear of a convoy of civilian cars was to be our only method of escorting people from their homes to the airport. A long way from ideal, but for now it was the best we could do.

In contrast to the first night, the roads were now full of people heading out of the city en masse. Mostly on foot, they had only left behind anything that couldn't be carried. All of the women were laden down like donkeys, balancing large bundles on their heads and carrying at least one other bag. The men on the other hand seemed to be carrying next to nothing and appeared happy to watch their women struggle. It was difficult to watch without passing judgment, but then I'd only been in Africa a week and a lot of what I saw appeared strange at first. Whether or not these people knew something we didn't or whether they were just being cautious we didn't know. And although there was a steady stream of them throughout the next few days, we stayed in our base, waiting for the order to move.

If it came, our job was to evacuate the French civilians and protect the French Embassy. Opposing the rebel forces was a job for the Congolese government and with the army now splitting along ethnic lines, it appeared that there were four or more different forces all vying for power. Keeping track of the fast moving political situation was difficult and would make any movement around town a nightmare…………impossible to tell the individual allegiance of the military units we came across. We did have direct communications with the French civilians though, who mostly lived together in the same upmarket area of town. This at least would alleviate the problem of crisscrossing all over the city picking up individuals.

The battles could be heard during the daylight hours but quite strangely, silence descended onto the streets as soon as night fell. It was as if there was an agreement that everyone clocked off at 5pm and went home, picking up where they had left off when they returned the following morning.

Stuck in base camp we made life as comfortable as possible and a week later we had managed to construct seats and a table out of bits of wood and pieces of bamboo hacked from the jungle. A shower had even been rigged up out of an old discarded piece of hosepipe. As much as making our base more habitable, all this DIY kept us busy and after the initial hype, we were in danger of dropping our guard. There was now even talk of packing our gear away and heading back to Gabon if the situation stabilised as it seemed to be doing. If the Congolese government continued to hold then we were told we'd be heading back in a less than a week.

I was disappointed at first that we'd flown this far, only to pack our bags and turn around. But the current stability inevitably meant that many hundreds or even thousands of civilian lives would be saved and we started to make preparations for our departure. We were even allowed to visit a local market that was still open to buy food to supplement our ration packs. And it was here that Tom and I met our first French civilians, who were also topping up on supplies.

'Bonjour'

Tom's hello was met by a snooty look by some toffy French bloke, who looked like he'd just trodden in something rather unpleasant. He simply dismissed Toms comment and moved on.

I found that to be incredibly rude and would have thought that having French troops here would have been a comforting thought.

But I was obviously wrong. Ah well....bollocks to him. If all the French civilians were like him then maybe it was better that we were going after all.

But with less than a day left, just as we'd got used to the idea that we were leaving and with some of the base already dismantled, the order came that the evacuation was back on. The government forces were losing ground and the safety of the French civilians could no longer be guaranteed. The rebels had set up road blocks essentially trapping the civilians in their homes. It would now be up to us to negotiate a way through....a sort of Mexican standoff with no side wanting to shoot first.

With the evacuations starting at first light, our team took its turn as the rapid reaction force. This entailed having two men on a roving guard, whilst the rest waited, fully kitted and ready to go at a second's notice. With nightfall I'd fitted the night scope to my sniper rifle and was busy checking everything was working when we received news of an ambush. A team had been on a late run from the airport and had been ambushed on the way back. It was difficult to get a clear picture of events but there were definitely casualties and they needed help.

'You three....get on the truck....you're escorting the ambulance'

Ducs grabbed extra rounds for the Minimi and we sprinted towards the waiting trucks that were already filled with most of the platoon. Valera helped me up and we sped off into night. There was one truck in front of the ambulance and ours at the rear. I could hear a fire fight raging in the distance and wondered if it was our guys. Not that automatic gunfire was unusual in this part of the world but it could be. We didn't know much of what we were heading into but all down the truck people were checking their weapons. Ducs had dispensed with the M16 magazines and had slapped a 200-round belt on instead. My night scope was working well and further down the truck Jim, the platoon medic, was checking his kit. The tension was intense as we headed towards the noise of the fire fight which still seemed like it was in full flow. My heart was pounding as the reality of the situation started to dawn. Whatever we were heading into, I just wanted to get it over with and pushed forward the bolt on my rifle, putting a round into the chamber.

'....WATCH OUT....ENEMY LEFT....'

A second later there was a sound like heavy hail landing on a steel roof and bees buzzing past your ears as enemy bullets sprayed the truck, bringing it to an instant halt. Not waiting for the command, we leapfrogged over the side, landing in a heap before sprinting to a ditch on the opposite side of the road. Chaos reigned as people fell over each other trying to sort themselves into firing positions. Corporals were screaming above the noise of incoming automatic fire to make themselves heard and to regain command.

It looked like we'd arrived at the scene of the initial ambush and had driven headlong into the middle of a gun battle. Our small convoy, including the ambulance had been attacked, but by shear good fortune it looked like we'd escaped without injury.

The amount of incoming rounds was intense and it was obvious we were outnumbered. With the adrenaline pumping and without taking any real aim I quickly squeezed off a couple of rounds in the general direction of the enemy, whilst at the same time trying to expose as little of my body as possible above the protection of the ditch. With the street lamps lit up, the night sight became next to useless, returning the rifle to an outdated single shot bolt action, surrounded by modern automatic weapons. I heard Ducs open up with the Minimi at the enemy, who were located on the far side of the main road, and where protected by a small wall and a few buildings. Its high rate of fire sounded reassuring and after the initial few seconds of confusion, our response started to seem more organised.

Orders were shouted out directing our fire and a quick head count was taken. We were one man down; he was still trapped in the first vehicle. He had been driving one of the trucks but had been left behind when we'd sprinted for the ditch. Hopefully he was only wounded, and one of the pathfinder platoon volunteered to race across no-man's-land and bring him back.

A call went out for covering fire and we opened up with everything we had as the French corporal, ducking and weaving like a madman, sprinted into the enemy fire. The noise of the fire fight was deafening as we tried to keep the enemy's heads down by throwing as much lead at him as possible. It looked like a wall of red tracer rounds was going towards the enemy, but a few metres before the truck, the corporal appeared to stumble and fall. I half expected him to get back onto his feet, but instead, he stayed on the ground....motionless. I don't think anyone doubted for a second that he was dead. Not that we were experts....but there was something intuitive in the way he lay that just said he wasn't getting up again.

But this was not the time to reflect, and an Irish sergeant immediately volunteered to make a second attempt. The order came out again for more covering fire and with another hail of fire the sergeant rose from cover and sprinted towards the truck. His 6-foot frame presented a huge target, but showing incredible courage he made it to the truck and yanking open the door, pulled the driver free. Pausing only long enough to throw him over his shoulder, he then managed to make the return journey unscathed. The driver, who was unconscious, had been shot in the head and the doctor immediately went to work on him trying to stabilise his condition.

The enemy fire seemed to be reducing in intensity, and crouching down to change the magazine on my rifle I saw Mike lying on his back gasping for breath. Mike was a Kiwi and his easy-going nature had made him an extremely popular member of the company. He had been part of the original patrol that had been ambushed and had crawled up to our position to pass on a message. With everyone concentrating on what was happening in front of us, no one had noticed him. He had blood pouring from his face where a round had hit him just below the jaw. Jim the platoon medic jumped to his aid, pulling his helmet off to get a better look at the injury. There was an exit wound on the opposite side of his face but so much damage had been caused that his windpipe had become blocked, making it almost impossible for him to breathe.

'....Shit....the fuckin' medic kit is on the truck....'

In the initial panic Jim had instinctively grabbed his rifle but had forgotten the medic kit. But without a word he sprinted out of the ditch and raced towards the truck, zigzagging like a rabbit dodging a pack of dogs.

'....APC....DEAD AHEAD....'

Valera slapped a rocket onto the end of his FAMAS and without taking any real aim fired it in the direction of the enemy. It slammed into the front of the APC as it tried to exit from a gated entrance. The APC was a South African model, originally designed for riot control and was more of an armoured truck than an Armoured Personnel Carrier. The small rocket hit the engine and exploded with a huge bang and a small cloud of smoke, bringing the truck to a standstill. Another slammed into its side at almost point blank range and left it smoking and stationary. Jim had shown incredible bravery retrieving his medical kit in the middle of all this, but the only thing that could save Mike now was what he could do with it. The rest of us felt completely useless and could only offer what help was needed. We'd all done a basic first aid course, but there was a huge difference between that and the injuries Mike had. He needed someone who knew a lot more than how to put a field dressing on someone.

Mike was now choking on blood, broken bits of bone, flesh and anything else that had blocked the back of his mouth. His face was a mess and Jim started pushing a tube up his nose, trying to get a passageway down into his lungs. But time after time Mike kept pushing it away. He was a strong guy and unless he allowed Jim to help him it was never going to work. Although Mike was conscious he couldn't speak and the lack of progress was unbearable.

'....Mike....you've got to let me help you mate....I can't do anything unless you help me....'

Jim was getting anxious....They were mates and he new he could save him. But in an incredible show of personal courage, Mike started writing with his finger, in a mixture of blood and mud, on a piece of cardboard.

'....Not breathe....let me....'

Together they started again with Jim pushing the tube and Mike stopping to make small adjustments until the tube was in place.

It was one of the toughest things I'd ever seen and I was astounded at Mike's bravery. And with at least a small airway now open, Jim attached a dressing to Mike's face and placed a drip into his arm.

Whilst some of the platoon pushed through the enemy's position, Fino and I were allocated to sorting out what vehicles could still be used. We started with the ambulance and apart from suffering two flat tyres and a few bullet holes, it seemed OK. The rest of the trucks were also still capable of running and so we set about loading our dead and wounded. As for the enemy, they were either dead or had retreated, but not wanting to hang around any longer than necessary, we started back towards our base.

The city seemed even more silent than usual as we moved slowly through the streets and the only sound to be heard was the….thud, thud, thud of the ambulance running on flat tyres. It was a horrible sound and watching it made me think of a wounded beast limping back to its home.

The camp was on full alert and had been waiting for our arrival. The medical centre had also been alerted to our casualty situation and was waiting to take over. Apart from Mike and the driver, there were two others seriously wounded and a number of others who had minor cuts. I hadn't seen the enemy positions, but from those who had, their accounts varied from between 10 and 20 dead.

It was pretty obvious that our lack of proper armoured vehicles had exposed a weakness that the enemy had taken advantage of. The atmosphere in the camp was now one of wanting to get out there and take the fight to them. The trouble was that we didn't know who the enemy were and it wasn't our job to fight them anyway. Frustrating as it was, our mission was to evacuate the French civilians…..not to get dragged into the middle of a civil war.

There were lessons to be learnt though and the following day we re-distributed our ammunition and set about getting what vehicles we did have as well armoured as possible. Extra flak jackets were secured in position so as to protect the driver as much as possible. If we were to drive though any ambush in future, we'd at least stand a better chance of survival. We also heard that a couple of our Armoured Vehicles were due to be flown in from France. But it was sad and ironic to think that the plane that would fly them in would be leaving with our dead and wounded.

I was on guard later that night and I was thinking of how Mike would have died if it hadn't been for Jim. With the doctor taking care of the driver there is no way we would have coped without him. His knowledge had impressed me before and I decided that when we got back to France I'd volunteer for the Medics course. It would be difficult to pass, requiring a good understanding of French and would mean four months away from the regiment. But if I ever found myself in that situation again, there was no way I wanted to feel that useless. The next time I wanted to know what to do.

A couple of hours later and still on guard, I switched the night vision goggles on to peer down the jungle path. My guard position involved patrolling a 200 metre stretch of the perimeter and most of it was along a narrow trail through the thick jungle. The night goggles worked on the same principle as the night scope on my rifle, magnifying any available light source which turned everything into shades of green. But with the thick jungle canopy drowning out all light they weren't working too well. The view was now one of either dark green or black, which didn't really help at all and so after fiddling with the focus I decided I'd be better off without them. Besides, using them for any length of time destroyed your natural night vision, leaving you almost blind for a few minutes after switching them off.

I made my way slowly down the trail, walking no more than a few metres at a time before stopping, dropping to one knee and listening out. It's amazing how much information our senses can pick up in these situations and how much more aware of our surroundings we become. It took a lot of concentration to keep focused, but 50 metres down the trail I heard a rustle in the undergrowth, outside of the perimeter and away to my right. Instinctively dropping to one knee I strained to listen for any more sound. There is was again, only clearer this time and more distinctive.

There was definitely someone walking though the jungle towards me. The jungle was thick and made an unmistakable sound when brushed past. Whoever it was also knew what they were doing. They would move a metre or so, stop and listen for a few minutes and then move off. They obviously knew how to travel through the jungle at night and they seemed to be heading in my direction.

I was frozen to the spot for a second while I weighed up my options, which seemed to take me forever but probably took no more than a few seconds. Calling on the radio was not an option as it would instantly give my position away and for the time being that was to my advantage. In fact having the radio switched on at all could give me away and so I turned it to mute. Turning back around and letting someone walk straight into our camp was not on either and nor was continuing to move forward. It fact, making too much movement in any direction could give my location away.

To the left of the path, no more than a few metres away and directly in line with the oncoming enemy there was a thick tree root that almost looked like an armchair. If I could wedge myself in there, I would at least be in the shadows and the thick roots would offer me a bit of protection from the sides. Crawling on all fours as slowly as possible, I made my way to the tree and as quietly as I could, sat back against the moss covered root. I was now in a sitting position and if nothing changed would meet the enemy as he broke though the undergrowth about two metres in front of me. Not exactly a standard fire position, as from the front the whole of my body was exposed, but it was the best I had.

I pulled my rifle close in by my side so that I'd be almost firing from the hip. At no more than two metres there would be no need to take aim and at least this way I was comfortable and could concentrate more on listening for his movements. My sniper rifle could well prove to be my Achilles' heel, as it was designed for long range. My opponent would no doubt be armed with an AK47 that would squirt out a hail of bullets with a single compression of the trigger. I would only have time for one shot and so it needed to count. I thought about a head shot, but even at this short distance I was worried about missing and so decided to aim at his chest. It was strange to think that I'd been hitting head shots in practice at over 400m but here I was worried about missing at less than two metres.

I listened intently and could hear him getting closer. I was sure that my senses had never been as finely tuned as they were now. My body seemed to instinctively switch off everything that wasn't necessary to keep me alive, and turn up the receptiveness of those that were. I can't remember being scared. Not that I was particularly brave, I just think that my natural survival gene kept squashing any thoughts of fear because it knew they wouldn't help me.

I slipped the safety catch off and let my finger slowly rest on the hair line trigger that would take no more than the slightest of pressures to fire. I could hear my heart pounding in my chest and for some bizarre reason, figured that he must be able to hear it as well. So I started breathing though my open mouth, which ridiculously, seemed to me to make less noise. With the enemy no more than three or four metres away my head twitched when I heard another movement in the jungle.

Shit....there's two of them....Bollocks!....now I'm really fucked.

Of course there were two of them. Why wouldn't there be. No one in their right mind would try and attack on their own. I couldn't believe how stupid I'd been. But my mind must have somehow computed the best idea because I just seemed to instantly decide on a plan.

Shoot the first guy as soon as he appeared through the jungle. Turn towards the second. And at the same time, pull back the bolt, eject an empty round, push the bolt forward and fire again.

That was it....probably a shit plan....but that was it.

I placed my index finger on the trigger, allowing my first finger to rest underneath the bolt, giving me that extra millisecond that could make all the difference. Staring hard I started to see the undergrowth move. This was it....just stick to the plan and hope for the best....

The leaves parted and my hands gripped tighter on the rifle as I could see movement behind the dense foliage. I didn't want to shoot too early and miss. I had to wait until I could see him and held my breath as he finally broke through onto the trail.

It's a DOG....a fucking Great Dane with big dopey eyes staring straight at me. Where the fucking hell did a Great Dane come from in middle of the Congo? I'd seen little cross breeds running around....but this was proper full breed, Scooby Doo of a Great Dane.

I couldn't believe I'd gone through all of that over a dog. I suppose I was relieved in a way but looking at my watch realised I was five minutes late for the guard change. Although I'd been sitting there for over an hour it had felt like no more than two minutes. Grabbing my gear I ran back down the trail and emerged to find Fino looking around.

'Where've you been?....Is the radio broke?....I've been calling you and everything?'

'Don't ask mate....I really can't be bothered trying to explain'

Completely knackered, I wandered back to the sleeping area, hoping to get my head down for a few hours only to find Alf conducting a bag search. My heart sank....Oh God....what's he up to now?

Alf, our glorious team leader had asked everyone if they had a spare water bottle and machete, but not liking the negative responses had decided to look for himself. Being Alf though, when deciding on what bits of kit to bring to the Congo, he had managed to pack his full parade uniform, including ceremonial epaulettes and blue sash. Not that they had been on the packing list mind. And as you can imagine for an operational tour, you didn't need much common sense to tell you that a water bottle might prove useful. But then common sense wasn't Alf strongest point and after the last couple of days I couldn't help laughing at the big daft bastard. It might sound a little suicidal under the present circumstances, but even here I was still grateful he was our team commander. To my mind it was better to have a good hearted, although slightly incompetent team leader, than a competent, nasty little weasel.

After another day back in base camp we found ourselves back in our converted 4x4's, heading towards the upper class suburbs of Brazzaville that housed the French civilians. The evacuation was in full swing now, but with a shortage of armoured personnel carriers (APC's), it was still proving to be a fairly slow process. Convoys of local civilian cars would be escorted with our APC taking the lead and our other vehicles located in the middle and rear. Any civilians who didn't have cars would most likely catch a lift or be crammed into the back of the APC. The whole convoy would then move towards the airport passing through road block after road block, all of which were manned by different rebel groups and needed to be negotiated through. Mostly there wasn't a problem, because I think most of the groups just wanted to see the back of the civilians as soon as possible so that they could then ransack their homes for the rich pickings.

As we sped through the city in the middle of the afternoon heat, we rounded a corner and seeing a road block, I slammed on the brakes. Immediately suspecting an ambush I selected reverse and stood hard onto the throttle causing the pickup to wheel spin as we shot off back down the road. Coming to a halt some distance away I looked at Alf for orders and could see his head buried in the map.

'Shit....That's the only way through!'

With myself and Ducs staying with the pickup offering covering fire with the Minimi and sniper rifle, Alf led Valera, Rocky, Fino and Jacques back towards the road block. They swept through the area, ensuring it was clear before signalling for us to join them.

The road block had been constructed out of dead bodies lain across the middle of the street. And with the rest of the team in defensive positions, it was down to Ducs and I to clear a way through. I suppose we could have driven over them and Alf did offer us the option, but neither of us had been here long enough to be that disrespectful and dismissed the idea out of hand. Driving over dead people just wasn't on. Besides, it seemed like they'd already suffered enough whilst still being alive to at least deserve a little dignity in death. Not that being dragged into the gutter could be described as dignified, but it was better than being driven over.

The first guy was missing a head and I could still make out the fresh machete cuts on his neck. His flesh was still red, indicating that he'd not been there long. But strangely there was no sign of his head. He'd also soiled himself and I started gagging as I dragged his body onto the grass verge. The second guy was lying on his back with his hands still stretched out above his head. His pants were by his ankles; exposing his genitals which looked liked they'd been hacked at with a machete. His upper body and head were shiny and pink as if he'd then been set alight, or as if he'd been left out in the sun too long. An expression of sheer terror was etched into his face. It was a disgusting sight, but with Ducs rolling another body out of the way we managed to make a space wide enough for the pickup to squeeze through.

Driving on towards the suburbs no one spoke. Seeing dead people hadn't bothered me. But seeing the sheer inhumanity that people showed towards each other as the society broke down was just depressing. Not liking someone is one thing, but chopping some stranger's head off in the middle of the street is something else. But maybe I was just being naïve, and maybe it shouldn't have come as any great surprise. I guess I wasn't the first person to realise, that life here seemed so much cheaper!

The outer suburbs took me a little by surprise with their wide tarmac roads, Spanish style villas and perfectly manicured lawns. They contrasted the corrugated iron roofed, hand built shacks that most of the locals seemed to live in, which had open sewers that stank in the claustrophobic heat of the sun. You would have thought they were thousands of miles apart from one another, not just a few hundred feet. But the civilians seemed genuinely pleased to see us as we blocked one end of the street and set about forming the convoy.

Pulling the pickup across the centre of the road, I got out and placed the sniper rifle on the bonnet. There was anxious commotion and heated exchanges behind me as the officers negotiated with a family to unload some of their possessions to make room for an extra passenger. Considering that there was sitting room only on the plane it seemed ludicrous that some people were still trying to take pot plants and all sorts of rubbish with them. Most of the civilians had families, and their crying children only added to the tension. Someone from another vehicle started gobbing off to hurry things up and within minutes it looked like a scene from an Italian traffic jam with everyone shouting at each other.

I turned away, leaving the company commander to negotiate a peace and get things moving. And as I looked back down the road, a brand new BMW saloon with blacked out windows and loud music blearing out sped past the entrance to the road at high speed....followed a few moments later by a similarly menacing looking Mercedes. They passed out of sight and for a second I didn't think there was anything to worry about....until they turned around and came cruising back up the road.

With the music still blaring out, they crawled to almost a stand-still before stopping five metres or so away from my position.

'What do you reckon?'

Fino was standing at the back of the pickup and was as alarmed as I was.

'Not sure yet'

I pulled the shoulder stock of the rifle into my shoulder as the back window lowered to reveal three guys dressed in a mixture of civilian and military clothing. The guy nearest the window had a shaven head, more gold necklaces than Mr.T and was wearing a black vest that showed off his pumped up physique. He looked at me through his jet black lifeless eyes and smiled, exposing a row of gold teeth. Holding an Uzi sub machine pistol in one hand, he looked more like a New York gang member than a rebel fighter. His mate passed him a joint that he drew heavily on, casually blowing the sweet-smelling marijuana smoke towards me with all the confidence of an untouchable Mafia boss.

Unfortunately for him, his driver had stopped so that my rifle was pointing directly at him. But he seemed completely unphased and never losing my stare, finished off his joint as if he had all the time in the world, before closing the window and moving off down the street.

I guess for him this was the real prize of the military coup. With no law and order to speak off, those with guns could do whatever they wanted. I'm sure that all they were waiting for was for us to leave so they could be first on the scene. These were the richest houses in the city and once empty would be easy pickings. They knew it as well as we did, and I guess the last thing these guys were interested in would be getting into a fight with French soldiers. Once we were gone, their only problem would be trying to transport everything!

The convoy was slowly taking shape and I was called over and told to drive a people carrier that the owners didn't feel safe driving through the city. The father I instantly recognised as the toffy bloke who had looked down his nose at Tom in the market.

'Hello there'

His response to me could not have been more polite and I was thinking about having a dig about his previous attitude, but he recognised me and looked away a little embarrassed. It was ironic to think that the people he didn't think worthy of speaking to a few days ago, where now the same people he was asking to drive his family to safety. But that's probably the same for soldiers from any army. Half of the time they are being slammed as drunken hooligans on a Saturday night, and the rest of the time hailed as liberators.

The toffy bloke sat in the front and his wife and their two small children climbed into the back. His wife was typically French, being perfectly dressed with short dark hair, a petite frame and an accent that could melt stone. She chatted to me for a minute and I realised that this was the first proper face-to-face conversation I'd had with a female since I'd join the Legion. It was wonderful and for a moment I completely forgot where I was. There was also another couple catching a lift, and they looked more petrified than everyone else. Both were in their thirties, and the woman was obviously French. But her husband was a local man and although they were married, he didn't have a French passport. Technically speaking this meant that he couldn't get on a plane and shouldn't even have been in the convoy. But it was not up to us to make those decisions and we let him come along. With places on the military planes limited, it would be up to the officials at the airport to decide whether or not to let him board.

After what seemed like hanging around for ages and with the vultures either circling or waiting in the shadows for us to go, we slowly pulled away in a long convoy and headed off in the direction of the airport. The whole area was deadly quiet and we were forced to slow down to pass through the dead body road block. The French mother covered her children's eyes to protect them from the sight, but the other French lady just buried her head in her husband's chest and starting weeping. They both knew what could happen if he wasn't allowed on that plane, without this to act as a graphic reminder. But it certainly brought home the importance to the rest of us, because up until that point I'd never really thought about just how valuable a passport could be. Passing through the road block we continued at our painfully slow pace until we turned onto one of the main roads into the city centre and came across a manned road block.

Whilst the Captain negotiated with the rebels or government forces or whoever it was that was manning this particular road block, we sat nervously and waited with the engine ticking over. No more than ten metres away on the side of the road was the road block's forward position. A small protective wall had been built out of sandbags and a Rocket Propelled Grenade (RPG) was resting on the top, pointing directly at us. The soldier was wearing sunglasses and his dreadlocks were hung casually to shoulder length. The Rastafarian look was completed by his faded Bob Marley t-shirt and with his finger resting on the trigger, he was unnerving the hell out of the whole car.

It was the unpredictability that was so unsettling. Because who knew whether he was drunk or drugged up, and fancied blowing away a car of civilians just to brighten up his day. This was not exactly a well disciplined army and we'd also discovered why there was significantly less fighting during the night. Most of the guys just partied in the evening, drinking and smoking drugs, wandering around the streets doing whatever they wanted to anyone unfortunate enough to be caught outside, and as a result most of the local civilians had already left the city for the countryside. But those with nowhere to go or who were incapable of making the journey, had started to congregate outside of our camp. Not allowed to enter, they had simply camped by the main gate and the whole place was now looking more like a refugee centre than a military base. Each day the population grew as word spread and although only a temporary stopgap, at least for the moment they were relatively safe. In truth, we probably compounded the situation by handing out ration packs in the absence of any organised aid relief. But there was no real alternative. You couldn't just let people starve on the side of the road by claiming that not handing out food would benefit the greater population in the long run.

Having passed safely through the road block we continued into the city centre that was now strewn with litter from its burnt out office blocks. The walls were peppered with shrapnel scars and they were still smouldering after having been set alight. The whole scene was an apocalyptic one where a large battle had obviously taken place. Reams of paper were still floating around in the thermals of warm air resembling a ticker-tape parade, and a civilian pickup truck converted to carry a heavy machine gun, was lying on its side with its wheel hanging off where it had been hit by an RPG. Our wheels crunched over the litter and empty cartridge cases, that were so thick they formed a carpet-like surface to drive over.

I could see the toffy bloke was getting agitated and he turned around to comfort his wife and children who were now clinging to their mother. This was their home and it must have been heartbreaking to see it in such a state. His tone sounded scared and he kept asking how much longer it would take. Not able to give an accurate answer I mumbled something ambiguous, but at the same time realised how lucky I was. All I had to worry about was me. And I could occupy myself by concentrating on the job and reassuring myself that I was well trained, I had good backup, I had good equipment, etc., etc. But having to sit here with your wife and two small children, worried that any second they could be taken away from you must have been a petrifying experience. It was truly humbling and I wouldn't have wanted to swap places with them for anything. But I could feel their mood calm a little as we broke out onto wider roads.

We passed a supermarket that was being looted and could see cars that were so overloaded their exhausts scraped on the floor. A couple of blokes were comically trying to manhandle one of the supermarket's large chest freezers onto the roof of a small saloon car. The fact that the freezer was bigger than the car didn't seem to be dampening their spirits and the French mother chuckled, which broke our awkward silence. Once onto clearer roads we picked up speed, leaving the city behind and arriving safely at the airport.

I'd not been here for a couple of days and the place was now crammed full of hundreds of civilians waiting to be flown out. There was also a Legion infantry regiment that had been flown in to take over the guarding of the airport. And there was a regular French Army Special Forces unit who were busy picking up supplies. Tasked with protecting the French Embassy they had been making daily trips to the airport, ferrying boxes of diplomatic papers out and bringing back food and water. There was a French Officer giving an interview to a film crew and I could see a number of other journalists mooching around taking photos.

The arrival of our convoy gave them something new to photograph and they made a bee line for us, treating us like mini celebrities for ten seconds, snapping away with their telephoto lenses and shoving micro-phones in people's faces. The toffy bloke refused an interview and they moved onto the next car where a mother was cradling a baby.

After helping my passengers with their few possessions, the French woman shook my hand, thanked me and wished me well. She and her family then disappeared into a crowd of civilians who had congregated around an official-looking building. The other couple were not looking so confident and I hoped that their troubles were not just about to start. Wishing them both the very best of luck I left them beside a hanger and drove off.

The overflowing car park had now extended into a field and by the time I'd returned, Ducs and Fino were busy loading our pickup with cans of Pepsi. They had found a crate full of them and had decided to claim a few cases before anyone else did. Lots of stuff had been flying into the airport over the last month, but with the ever worsening security situation, most of it was still in the hangers and would now be going nowhere. Rocky and Valera had managed to scrounge some fruit and with Alf away receiving orders, Jacques was busy trying to track down a particular brand of cigarette.

After leaving the APC and the other teams at the airport for another job we headed back to base camp on our own. With the sun fading, the humidity seemed to increase and our heavy flak jackets did nothing to cool us down. Our clothes were permanently damp and grimy with sweat and I was thinking about getting back and having a shower. Alf had managed to pick up some washing powder, so that for the first time since being here we'd be able to wash our clothes. And with the fresh fruit and Pepsi on board, we were all in high spirits as we sped back through the city.

There were still a few civilian cars on the road, driven by locals, and I was surprised when we came to a halt in a row of traffic.

'Road Block up ahead'

Ducs had a bird's eye view from the back of the pickup where he was manning the machine gun.

Alf shook his head and checked his map against a road sign. There shouldn't have been any road blocks on this particular route back to camp and he was double-checking we weren't lost.

Not being a great map reader I held my breath as Valera shouted from the back, asking whether everything was all right.

The good news was that we weren't lost and so the road block must have been set up in the last couple of hours. We stayed put, moving forward in the row of traffic until there were only a couple of cars ahead of us. I wasn't overly concerned as the cars seemed to be moving through quite quickly, and jumping the queue may well have only spooked the rebels. Given how trigger-happy they could be, that wasn't a good idea.

The car in front of us moved forward and the driver handed over a few papers to the guard. He was driving a bright red American convertible with white leather seats and chromed bumpers. His wife or girlfriend was sitting in the passenger seat and I was thinking how out of place it seemed. It was well looked after, but with the guard coming back with his papers, I put the pickup into first gear. Handing the papers back with one hand, the guard drew his pistol with the other, placed it next to the driver's temple and casually pulled the trigger.

There was a second of complete silence as everyone took in what had just happened. Time seemed to be moving in slow motion as my brain tried to catch up with the reality of the situation. No one was reacting, which meant that either no one knew what to do, or that he really had only pulled the trigger a second ago and it just seemed like we'd been sitting here for minutes.

The girlfriend's screams shattered the silence and brought me rushing back into reality. Covered in blood and with bits of brain in her hair, she fumbled with the door handle in panic before managing to open it. Standing in the road screaming the guard raised his pistol again, and at the same time I heard the sound of rifles being cocked in the back of the pickup. The sound caught his attention and glancing in our direction, his face dropped when for the first time he noticed we were there. But within a second his expression had changed from one of surprise, to one of panic, and finally to one of friendliness. He smiled at us as if we were his oldest friend he'd not seen in a long time.

'My friends....welcome'

His tone could not have been friendlier if he'd tried, and he raised his arms out as if to greet us.

'No one shoot until I say'

Alf couldn't see the rest of the team from the pickup's cabin and didn't want to start a shoot-out if it could be avoided. Apart from the guard with the pistol there were another couple of blokes with AK47's whose weapons were also pointed in our direction.

The girlfriend suddenly made her bid to escape and bolted off down the road passing our pickup, still in her bare feet and with her arms waving frantically above her head. One of the guards instinctively started to raise his rifle to drop her but thought better of it and lowered it back down. The tension mounted as we stood there in silence facing each other off. It reminded me of one of those western shoot-outs were everyone is waiting for someone

to make the first move. But our orders were clear. Do not fire unless fired upon.

With the pickup still in first gear, I lifted my foot off the clutch
and slowly moved around the convertible towards the road block.
The white leather seats had been sprayed bright red and the driver,
still clutching his papers in one hand, was slumped over the passenger's side. I drove up to the road block feeling very exposed, knowing that Alf and I would be the first targets if anyone lost their nerve
and started shooting.

I mounted the pavement in order to get around the road
block, passing within less than a metre of the guard. His beaming
smile revealed tobacco-stained teeth and he shrugged his shoulders in a sort of.... 'Hey don't blame me....I only work
here'....kind of gesture. He even had the brass neck to wish us a
safe journey, before waving us on our way. Since being in the
Congo it had always been difficult to tell the good guys from the
bad guys. But now I was starting to wonder whether there were
any good guys at all. But if there were....then they were keeping
a bloody low profile.

We drove back into the base past a group of nuns who were
now camped by the main gate, and parked up next to our makeshift
camp. We were all a little subdued after the events at the road block
and no one talked much as we unloaded our gear. It was now
getting dark and I was just about to get some sleep when Fino
invited me over for a cup of tea. I'd not had a cup of tea in months
and had to ask whether he was serious. But he'd managed to get
hold of some loose tea leaves and had manufactured a simple tea
strainer from a plastic bottle by punching some holes in the
bottom. It wasn't exactly sophisticated, but it did the job and the tea
tasted fantastic. Because if there was one thing I'd grown to miss
about home....it was a decent cup of tea.

The following morning we spent washing our clothes or sorting out any other bits of personal admin, before tucking into our
ration pack lunch. With only a limited number of menus, our
favourite pastime was now trying to get hold of something we'd
not had before. But the store man had given us crates of the same

menu and we were becoming sick of eating the same thing every day. A different menu had become a prized possession and could be swapped for or an extra piece of fruit, or a pack of American cigarettes. Which made a welcome change from smoking the cheap tobacco that we were being issued with.

After lunch I was chatting to Tom whilst we wandered back to our camp when a burst of machine gun fire came whizzing past us making a loud whooshing noise. We instinctively hit the ground as the rounds exploded into a stone wall behind us. The rounds were heavy calibre and were being fired from the outside of our perimeter. They were like small artillery shells and knocked huge lumps of rock off the wall. Probably one of the Russian made 12.7mm machine guns that we'd seen a number of around town. We waited for the first burst to finish before sprinting to our sleeping area where our flak jackets and helmets were kept.

'Hey....look at Simon'

Simon was an Irish corporal from another platoon who had broken his leg and was waiting to be flown back to Gabon. He was handicapped by his crutches, and Tom had noticed him racing as fast as he could towards us. With the heavy calibre machine gun rounds whizzing past him he must have been breaking the world record for running on crutches. It was hilarious to watch and we couldn't help laughing as he willed himself on.

'HURRY UP SI....you slow bastard....we can't wait all day for you....'

Simon launched his crutch at Tom in temper and came crashing to the ground next to us gasping for breath. After taking the piss out of Si for being out of shape, we picked up our gear and raced towards the defensive positions we'd prepared in the first couple of days. Tom headed towards a trench that was his forward position and I made my way to a small concrete building that was on the edge of the perimeter. Sprinting through the jungle a round hit a tree a few yards away, shattering the trunk and sending needle-like wooden shards everywhere.

I burst through the back door of the building to find Fino already in position crouching below a window. Alf, Ducs, Valera,

Rocky and Jacques followed minutes later and headed upstairs to their pre arranged positions.

'See if you can spot anything with the sniper rifle?'

Oh cheers Alf.

It would have to be me that pops his head above the parapet.

The building was taking hits and although the machine gun had a fairly slow rate of fire, the rounds sounded like sledgehammer blows on the outside wall. Fino placed his FAMAS on the window sill and let off a burst of automatic fire. I popped up, and staring down the scope strained to see something. But nothing looked out of place. There was a small clearing and then nothing but dense jungle. The machine gunner must have been firing blind in the general direction of the camp. Because unless he had a forward spotter walking the rounds onto the target, then it could be no more than hit or miss.

Dropping back down again I relayed my observations to Alf and a few seconds later could hear him radioing the captain.

'Stay put....keep down'

That was the first sensible thing Alf had said since we'd been in the Congo. And with the rate of fire slowing down, there was nothing else to do but keep our heads down. Tom's team was in a trench a few yards away and I could hear them repeating that they couldn't see anything either. I couldn't really see anyone making a frontal assault on our camp. That would have been suicidal. But with this type of attack they might just get lucky. And after a few minutes without any fire, we started to pick ourselves up and think about standing down.

Walking out of the back of the building we heard a burst of gunfire from Tom's trench, and shouting for us to join them. As we crawled towards their position they were saying something about having seen a couple rebels with AK47's running down the edge of the jungle. They had returned fire when challenged and were now in a small building about 400m in front of the trench. Tom's team commander wanted Ducs and I to stay in the trench with his Minimi gunner and the rest of the team to assault the building.

Orders were quickly issued whilst the assault team prepared themselves, getting rid of any bits of kit that would weigh them down. Water, ammunition and their first aid dressing was all they would need. Anything else was left in the trench. Buchy, the other Minimi gunner fired off a burst towards the building, which was answered with an AK being held out of the window and half a magazine sprayed in our direction.

The assault was to be something that I think most armies would recognise. Our three-man fire team consisting of two Minimi's and a sniper rifle would pour rounds onto the enemy position. At the same time the assault team would move up under cover of the jungle and attack from the right flank. Just before their attack went in we would switch our fire to the left-hand side of the building. It was something we had practised a thousand times and was a textbook attack. With the assault teams moving off I looked down the rifle scope and fired off a few rounds through the window into the blackness of the room. Unless they popped their heads out of the window we were never going to get a clear shot. The single-storey building was made of prefabricated concrete slabs which our rounds couldn't penetrate. We were side on to the building and I guessed there couldn't have been a way out of the far side or they would have been long gone. They could make a run for it out of the back door, but then they would have to cover 200m of open ground. No....they were trapped....and unless they started waving white flags....they were in a lot of trouble.

Buchy and Ducs continued to put small bursts of fire into the building whilst I kept on putting rounds through the open widow. But apart from their initial burst of fire, there hadn't been any movement at all. I couldn't help but think the whole thing looked like the final stance of Butch Cassidy and the Sundance Kid, where we were the Mexican soldiers, waiting to shoot down the two guys the moment they emerged from the 'hacienda.' It felt a bit like shooting fish in a barrel and there was something that just didn't feel right. It was strange. I'd not had any issues about firing back during the ambush. But this seemed somehow different. It was hard to explain. But it just didn't seem like a fair fight. I know that sounds daft, because being fair has nothing to do with it. And it probably wasn't the best time to be having an attack of consciousness; but it was just how I saw it. The rebels didn't usually carry any more than a single magazine each. This meant that if they were not already out of ammunition, they very soon would be. In fact, the irony of the whole thing was that the scene couldn't have resembled 'Camerone' more if we'd tried. There, it was Legionnaires who were held up in a farmhouse, heavily outnumbered, and who fought on until out of ammunition. But here it was the rebels who were playing the part of the heroic Legionnaires! It couldn't have been any more ironic!

With still no movement from the house we could see the assault team forming up and we prepared to switch our fire. They set off over the hundred or so metres of open ground in three teams of two, with one team moving whilst the other two gave covering fire until they were only ten yards from the building. A couple of grenades were hurled through the windows, exploding with a puff of smoke and low-pitched thud. My sights were aimed at the back of the house waiting to shoot anything that came out. But after an offer to surrender, one of the guys came stumbling out of the front door with his hands up.

Our prisoner was handed over to the company commander and we later learned that the other rebel had been killed by one of the hundreds of bullets we'd fired through the open window. With no clear shot and our bullets unable to penetrate the walls, it must have ricocheted off the back wall of the room. As for the prisoner, I've no idea what happened to him. We didn't exactly have a set-up for prisoners and I guess he must have been handed over to the government forces....or what was left of them. They were losing ground all the time and from what information we were getting, the only reason they were holding on at all, was due to the number of different rebel groups who were still fighting each other.

A couple of days passed by and we continued the painfully slow process of escorting the civilians safely to the airport. And when not on escort duty, we were usually on guard or catching up on sleep. I felt permanently tired and so wasn't in the best of moods when a night-time guard duty was sprung upon us.

I was having a bit of a moan to myself patrolling the perimeter when a civilian jeep driving down the road caught my attention. It was dark and although it didn't have its headlights on that didn't really surprise me. A lone car was an easy target at the best of times without drawing attention to it, and so it was better to take your chances with no headlights and hope you didn't hit anything. But when a minute later it came crawling back down the road, I started to get suspicious. I was only 20m or so from the road, but I was well hidden against the backdrop of the jungle and was confident they couldn't see me. I crouched down and watched as they turned around again and passed my position, going back in the opposite direction.

I spotted Ducs patrolling his sector and called him over. He had noticed the car as well and we decided to continue watching for a while before getting on the radio and letting Alf know.

Crawling forward through the undergrowth we managed to get ourselves into a good vantage position where we could see both ways down the road, but were still well hidden. There were no street lights which suited the night scope. Ducs had a pair of night vision goggles and it wasn't long before the jeep came back down the road and stopped about 50 metres in front of us next to an old shack. The driver got out and disappeared into the building before emerging a few moments later. Ten minutes later he was still sitting in the jeep, but because it was facing away from us I couldn't see what he was up to. There was definitely no light because even a cigarette would glow like a bright white dot on the night scope and he didn't seem to be speaking to anyone. It was very suspicious and only served to intrigue us all the more. Because unless you had a death wish, the one thing you defiantly didn't do in this city, was to take a nice quiet night-time drive on your own.

He was still there ten minutes later when we heard another car making its way slowly down the road. It came to a halt behind the jeep and a couple of blokes got out and started unloading stuff from the boot and transporting it into the shack. It was difficult to make out what it was, but it looked like rifle-shaped objects wrapped up in blankets. This wasn't such a big deal because over the last couple of days, practically everyone we met on the streets had a gun. The sensible option would be to leave for the countryside, but if you were going to stay in the city, then arming yourself seemed like a wise thing to do. The guy in the jeep was obviously buying weapons, which in Brazzaville was as easy as buying a loaf of bread, but I was puzzled when only one guy came back out and drove off in the car.

The two other guys came out a few minutes later, cradling their bounty and placing it in the back of the jeep, before starting to unwrap it. But rather than the rifle I'd first suspected, he pulled out an RPG, which even in Brazzaville was a bit over the top for home security. I pulled back the bolt slightly and double-checked I had a round in the chamber before closing it shut again. Ducs cocked the Minimi as quietly as possible and rested his finger on the safety catch. Adjusting the focus on the scope, I turned one of the switches which illuminated the cross hairs, making them glow bright red against the green background.

'I'll take the RPG....you take the other guy....'

Ducs nodded and pulled the Minimi into his shoulder. The RPG guy still didn't have a rocket attached and as long as that's how it stayed, there wouldn't be any bother. He seemed to be inspecting his buy and I couldn't quite figure out why they didn't just drive off. The driver got back behind the wheel whilst the RPG guy rummaged around in the back of the jeep, before he pulled out one the distinctive looking rockets. Fitting it into the end of the RPG he held it on his shoulder, whilst pointing it into the air. The RPG was now loaded and I could feel the adrenaline surging through my body. The RPG was a fairly crude weapon but devastatingly effective. It had been around for years and although its shaped charge couldn't penetrate modern armour, it could make a mess of most other vehicles. It was also light, quick to re-load and small enough to make it perfect for urban warfare.

The RPG guy walked up and down the road a little, almost showing off before returning to the jeep and dropping to one knee, facing our camp. I looked at Ducs and he gestured.... 'After you!' It seemed almost polite given the circumstances, but I knew what he meant. He wouldn't shoot until I'd fired. But the RPG guy still wasn't pointing the RPG at us. It was still on his shoulder pointing in the air. But he was definitely kneeling down in a firing position.

Should I take the shot or not? I didn't think I'd miss. He was no more than 50 metres in front of me and kneeling down he made a nice round target. With the cross hairs fixed on his chest I pushed the safety catch off and rested my finger back on the trigger. Should I wait a few seconds more until he lowered the RPG or fire now? Whilst he stayed in this position, there was no real danger. But then who was to say that if he fired it now it wouldn't act like a mortar round and come down in the middle of our camp? Or maybe even amongst the civilians that were camped by the main gate?

It was difficult to know what to do but I made the decision that unless he lowered it I wouldn't shoot. I decided that if he wanted to shoot at us then it would make more sense to lower it and fire!

He stayed motionless for a more seconds and I readied myself to pull the trigger. Half a second later Ducs would spray the driver with machine bullets and by the time I'd reloaded the whole thing would be over. But bizarrely he either lost his nerve or decided against the idea, because after kneeling there for a well over a minute he stood up and threw the RPG into the back of the jeep and jumped in. They drove off down the road and at the same time I heard Ducs let out a huge sigh.

'What the hell….was all that about?'

I was as stunned as he was and mumbled a reply. I was sure the guy was about to fire and couldn't believe that after all that he just got up and drove off. It wasn't even worth speculating as to his reasons. It just seemed an utterly strange thing to do. Maybe he had just bottled it….I don't know….and I guess I never will!

I rolled over and let out my own deflated sigh before picking myself up and heading back towards the guard position. These night-time guard duties had turned out to be nothing if not interesting.

Within a couple of days we had evacuated all of the civilians and had received orders that we would soon be following. The government forces were about to fall and some of our troops guarding the airport had already started to leave. We would dismantle our base here and then fall back to the airport, which by then would be the French Army's only presence in the country. Whilst the city was being fought over we would be guarding the airport, whilst our final personnel were evacuated from the country. Once completed, we would then be on the last aircraft out.

No French civilians had been injured and although we had suffered casualties, I suppose our mission could be counted as successful. Unfortunately the Congolese civilians had not fared so well and within hours of the news of our departure, the refugees who had gathered around our camp had started to pack up their belongings and move on. Most headed towards the countryside, no doubt in the hope of finding some other safe heaven. But one or two actually set off back into the city....hoping against hope to find sanctuary in the ensuing chaos.

We dismantled the camp within a day and started heading back to the airport, team by team. But I'd been told to drive the Company Sergeant Major, who would be one of the last to leave, and so was hanging around waiting for him and the Captain to close down the company HQ. I was impressed to see the Company Sergeant Major had chosen the same Lexus 4x4 that I'd driven when we'd been choosing cars at the airport. With no one to tell him what to pick he'd obviously decided that luxury would be the way to go. He had a huge French Tricolour taped to a pole that was flying from the rear window that made him look more like a football fan. And I was messing with the electric seats when there was a loud explosion about 20 metres away.

'MORTARS!....TAKE COVER!'

I sprinted into the Company HQ and took cover under an old table. The HQ had been made from one of the collapsed buildings and so offered a degree of protection from the flying shrapnel. Lying flat on the floor I heard another round land, followed shortly afterwards by another. The sound echoed around the small building and bits of plaster fell off the already collapsing walls.

After a couple more explosions, we took our chance and made a break for the vehicles. The Captain and his driver jumped into a jeep whilst the rest of us clambered into the Lexus with the final few pieces of gear. Some of our pathfinder platoon, who where still at the camp had been caught out in the open. They were already in their jeeps and stopped by our position, before we all headed towards the exit. I could hear more rounds landing, but didn't look back. The Land cruiser in front was kicking up clouds of dust and it was difficult to make out the road. Screeching to a halt by the main gate, we picked up the last two Legionnaires who were still on guard. Whoever had fired the mortars must have had a spotter in the jungle, signalling to open fire. One of our pathfinders had taken a piece of shrapnel in his back, but fortunately it didn't seem that serious. But with rebel fighters probably already pouring over our base, seeing what they could scavenge, we sped off towards the city at breakneck speed, not slowing down until we'd reached the main airport road and were clear of the suburbs.

Once we'd arrived at the airport, there were now no more French soldiers left in the city. All the French civilians that had wanted to be evacuated had been, leaving the airport as the only French foothold in the country. The place had changed again in the last couple of days and now looked almost deserted. The crowds of civilians had disappeared and there weren't as many TV crews or journalists to be seen. Most had no doubt got their story and had already moved on to the next headline. We'd spent a day driving some of them around the city and letting them out of our armoured personnel carriers to take photos. Most of them had shown incredible courage (or maybe naivety) and had been desperate to sit on top of the APC whilst travelling through the worst affected areas, just to get a few decent shots. This had made them easy targets and considering that only a few had flak jackets, I had to admire their bravery. Most were from the news agencies I'd heard of, like CNN or Reuters, but there were a few privately financed photo journalists. These guys seemed to spend their time touring the world's war zones, only able to make money when they managed to sell a picture. And a few were still at the airport, hanging on as long as possible in the hope of snapping a final few sell-able images.

Most of the Legionnaires from the other regiments had already packed their gear and were waiting near the runway to be flown out. This would leave a final force of around 200 paratroopers, which would be flown out in waves over the next four days.

The sides of the runway were now strewn with cargoes that had been dumped in an attempt to create more space for people on the planes. Some of it had been picked over, and after parking the Lexus, I spotted Fino rummaging though a couple of boxes.

'Found anything?'

'Na....Well....not unless you're pregnant!'

There were boxes and boxes of disposable nappies, powdered baby milk, sanitary towels and every other toiletry you could think of. In fact, the guy who finally got his hands on this lot would be able to open a chemist's shop five minutes later. But we were after food and drink, and as neither could be found, we helped ourselves to tube of toothpaste each and headed off. The platoon had been split up on arrival and was already dotted around the airport. Asking Fino where our position was, he just pointed towards the air traffic control tower and shook his head.

'What!....Alf's in charge of the air traffic control tower?'

'Oh yeah....'e's up there now getting a quick lesson on how it all works!'

This couldn't be true. Who in their right mind had decided to make Alf the air traffic controller? This I had to see. And as we climbed the stairs I imagined Alf sitting in front of a control desk, utterly confused by the flashing lights and coloured switches, but trying to convince us that he understood everything.

'No one is to touch anything....Absolutely nothing....I'm the only one who knows how it works....so only I'm allowed to do anything....Is that clear?'

'Oui Sergeant'

Alf's nose always started to twitch whenever he got confused and at the moment it looked like a radar dish moving in continuous circles. He didn't have a clue how anything worked and wasn't convincing anyone. Alf was a good bloke and in many ways an excellent soldier. He always pushed himself to the limits and whilst in Calvi, during our training runs in full kit, he always finished in the top three or four. Not because he was the fittest, but because he was the most determined. And we respected him for that. But there were things he just couldn't get to grips with. Map reading was one, anything more than basic tactics was another and now a couple of radios and a telephone could also be added to the list. To be fair, Brazzaville airport is not exactly Heathrow and the control tower could never be described as state of the art. But even so, Alf had obviously forgotten everything he'd been told five minutes earlier, because the colour drained from his face when a call came in over the intercom.

Valera started laughing to himself as Alf turned around and started talking into a headset that was attached to the desk. He received no response and started cursing the pilot for not answering, but a moment later the pilot's voice could be heard again asking for permission to land. Alf's stress levels were rising and he now began blaming the radios for not working. With the pilot making a third attempt to contact us, he looked like he was about to rip the headset out of the desk, when Valera pointed out he might try pressing one of the buttons in order to be heard. Not that making contact actually made the situation any clearer for the pilot, because after a two-minute conversation with Alf, he just seemed really annoyed and signed off with a very indignant….'I'm landing!'

The plane was an old Dakota C47 transport aircraft and would have been more at home in a museum. The Dakota had been the workhorse of the American army during the Second World War and had achieved aviation fame as the plane that was used to drop thousands of paratroopers during D-Day and Operation Market Garden. And as this one taxied down the runway, still painted in army green, it looked more like a battle re-enactment than real life. But it did represent much about what I'd seen so far in Africa. That nothing ever appeared to be thrown away or scrapped whilst it still worked. Even when things broke down and no longer worked, another use could always be found.

I was reminded again of this ability to re-use old military hardware the following day whilst I was on guard, on top of the air traffic control tower. Alf had decided that Valera and Rocky would stand watch over the control panel, leaving Ducs, Fino, Jacques and I to man the other two guard positions. This meant an absolutely knackering rota of two hours on, two hours off. And as we were only allowed to sleep between 10pm and 6am, once we'd taken off time for guard changes, we were down to three hours sleep per night. We weren't due to be flown out for another four days and I was counting down the time as I sat on the roof of the control tower looking out towards the surrounding hills. I saw of couple of truck movements about fifteen hundred metres away and used the binoculars to take a closer look. One of the trucks was a Second World War Russian rocket launcher and when it stopped, it just looked to be facing another hill. I had a brilliant vantage point though and following the direction of the truck I could see troop movements on a soft open slope about a kilometre in front of it.

The rocket launcher I recognised from TV documentaries and although officially known as a Katyusha rocket launcher, it had also been given the name of 'Stalin's Organs' due to the harrowing sound made when fired. Each truck carried 24 of the rockets and I could clearly make out soldiers around the truck preparing it for firing. It was incredibly compelling to watch and I quickly switched to look at the intended targets, who obviously had no idea of the devastation that was about to be brought down on them. Their position might have been exposed, but it had excellent views over the airport and I presumed that one of the final battles was about to begin. Because once we'd left, the airport would be a key position. Those that had control of the airport would also have control of the transport in and out of the country.

I could see that the soldiers on the hillside had dug in, but they were wandering around when I heard the loud screeching sound of one of the rockets being fired. I could easily follow its path through the air and watched as it landed in the middle of the hillside. The soldiers dived for cover as ten more rockets were fired almost simultaneously, churning the hillside into a mass of flying earth.

Within a few seconds the whole thing seemed to be over. The dust and smoke slowly moved off the hillside, leaving it looking like an acne-scarred face. And although it was too far away to hear anything, I could clearly make out a few bodies that weren't moving and could only imagine the sound being made by those who'd been wounded. I'd never seen artillery being used on exposed infantry before and it was a terrifying sight. It had been over almost before it had started, but within that short space of time had been utterly devastating.

Looking back at the truck it was making a rather slow retreat, but even so there was no return of fire from the soldiers on the hillside. It might have been well over fifty years old, but even today, despite its simplicity and crudeness, it still made it a fearsome weapon.

The fire fights continued over the next couple of days but never seemed to escalate into full scale battles. A light tank might role up, fire a few shots and then back off, or a jeep full of soldiers would fire five or six RPG rounds before retreating. Nothing was ever co-ordinated, but then I suppose with their limited resources, the logistics of war were dictating how the battles were being fought. The city was also still being fought over and smoke could be seen hanging like thick smog in the hazy heat. But with most of our gear already flown out, our unit was now reduced to just over a hundred.

With only a day left I was looking forward to getting back to Gabon, when the Legion decided to do what only the Legion could. A French Army General had decided that he was going to fly in on the last day and shake a few hands for a job well done. And although this was a little bit annoying; it wasn't that much of big a deal. All we had to do was to nod in the right places, and answer the standard question that senior officers always asked us, of what country we came from. This was the French Foreign Legion though, and they did have a habit of doing things differently. It was decided that there was to be a small guard of honour to welcome him off the plane and Alf had very kindly offered my services. We were to stand on the runway, fully exposed to anyone wanting a bit of free target practice, and wait for the General.

The little Spanish Sergeant in charge of the six-man guard of honour wasn't trying to hide the fact that he was annoyed and was cursing the General underneath his breath. He was getting restless and moaning at what we called the 'sketch' value, which was common language amongst Legionnaires when referring to anything that was done 'just for show.' And this was a classic example of how 'the show' was more important than 'the practical.'

As he paced up and down waiting for the General's plane, which could now be seen as a small dot in the sky, a bullet kicked up a piece of the tarmac and came to a rest next to his boot. It appeared to have dropped straight out of the sky and didn't seem to be travelling all that fast. But even so, it caused him to start cursing the Legion even more, as well as the stupidity of its officers. And I don't think that anyone disagreed with him; it's just that we weren't allowed to say anything. At least it had answered that age-old question of whatever happened to all those bullets you see being fired into the air on newsreel clips. And in the end our guard of honour was for nothing anyway, because the General walked straight past us giving the curtest of salutes, before jumping into the safety of a waiting armoured personnel carrier.

A day later we had left the air traffic control tower and were gathered on the side of the runway for a quick de-brief. The intensity of the fighting had increased during the morning and mortar rounds were now being fired over the airport. The rebels knew we were about to leave and each group was desperate to ensure that they would be first in. The sides of the runway were still littered with dumped cargoes and there was even a pallet of brand new French Army flak jackets that had been left behind. We were ordered to take what could carry and leave the rest.

Our final order was to take what we wanted from the Duty Free shop. Ten minutes after we'd flown out it would be ransacked anyway. So we were given permission to take as much as we wanted, provided it could be fitted into our rucksacks. (It wouldn't be the best piece of PR to see us walking off the plane in Gabon, laden down with armfuls of booze.) The shop was full of boxes of spirits, cases of beer and packets of cigarettes. But with the beer too bulky to carry, I helped myself to a couple of bottles of brandy and 600 cigarettes. It was bizarre really, because the airport manager had opened the shop and almost invited us to help ourselves. Whether he'd preferred us to take it rather than the rebels I don't know, but he was incredibly helpful. In fact I was surprised that he was still at the airport at all, because the small number of Congolese government troops that had been manning a heavy machine gun by the main entrance, had disappeared during the night.

Carrying all our kit on our backs, we waddled onto the waiting Transal. Its engines were still running and we'd started boarding as soon as the tailgate was lowered. I slumped into the cargo net seats and dumped the extra bits of kit on the floor. With no more than forty or so people on board there should have been plenty of room, but the extra gear still made it feel cramped. Even so, within a couple of minutes of landing the tailgate was being raised and we were taxiing back onto the runway. The sound of the engines revving in preparation for take-off felt familiar and comforting. The whole aircraft started to shake and I knew that within a couple of seconds, the brakes would be released and we'd be airborne almost immediately.

In many ways I had mixed emotions about leaving The Congo. It had been an incredible experience. It had been exciting, frightening, rewarding, sad, depressing, and uplifting all at the same time. And although I was glad to be leaving, there was a small part of me that would miss it; but I was looking forward to getting back to Gabon, with its hot showers, cold beer and real food. I was also looking forward to the Jungle Commando School that we should be starting within a couple of weeks. But we would soon learn that would have to wait, as within a couple of days we'd find ourselves flying into yet another African hotspot.

076

Deja Vu

The Barracks in Gabon felt luxurious after a month in The Congo and although we initially had to be housed in tents, it still felt like five-star treatment. We spent most of the first day cleaning our kit and handing it back into the stores before we were allowed to wash and clean ourselves. But by the end of the second day everything was squared away, and a few of us were chilling out in the hospital with a case of beer. We'd come to see Si who'd been stuck here with his broken leg and we figured he'd prefer some beers rather than a bunch of grapes. He was glad to see some familiar faces after having been trapped here since returning from The Congo a week earlier. We also gave him a bottle of whiskey and 200 cigarettes, courtesy of the duty free shop.

Tom was busy rolling his own smokes by the window and Jim was sitting on the end of the bed necking his fifth bottle in as many minutes, when Cowhead came into the room and told us the Colonel wanted to speak to us all, which was unusual in that the Colonel never spoke to us. The normal chain of command meant that the Colonel would usually speak to the Company Commander....and he might speak to us. But even he would normally speak to the Platoon commanders, who in turn would pass the orders onto us. So to have the Colonel of the Regiment speak to us was strange indeed, and we speculated as to what it might be.

The Colonel had proved exceptionally popular amongst the Legionnaires since taking command of the Regiment a year or so earlier. He was bit more 'gung ho' than his predecessors and his pragmatic approach had made him popular with us. It wasn't that he ignored tradition; it was just that he also kept one eye on the future. And so it was no surprise, when we paraded half an hour later on the football pitch, that he told us to break ranks and gather around.

We huddled around informally while he thanked us for our efforts in The Congo and how he knew we were looking forward to resting up in Gabon. It was one of those conversations where you were just waiting for the 'But,' and this one came in the form of The Central African Republic.

The country had been under the control of one military dictatorship after another, and during the 1960's and 1970's had famously had a self-titled 'Emperor', who had spent millions of the country's wealth on his on grandiose coronation. He had been eventually overthrown in the early 1990's and a democratic coalition government had been in power since 1993. But they had also been accused of corruption and in 1996 a mutiny by army leaders, who'd not been paid in months, had led to wider insurrection. This was initially put down with help from France, but by the end of the year, there was renewed fighting in and around the capital Bangui, between rebel and French forces.

The situation had calmed for a while when troops from neighbouring countries had taken over. But within the last week this 'peace-keeping' force had shelled a rioting Bangui, resulting in the death of over 100 and causing thousands to evacuate the city. Our job was to fly in and protect strategic locations around the country. There would be no evacuation of French civilians this time. This time we would be assisting the government in holding onto power.

We'd be flying out within 24 hours and so the priority would now be to collect all the kit we'd just handed back into the stores. That meant we'd have been back in Gabon less than three days, and most of us immediately busied ourselves with sorting out our personal kit whilst we had time. Within an hour or so, ammunition and stuff would start to be issued, and then any chance of getting on top of our personal admin would be out the window. Knowing that the place would soon become chaotic with people like Cowhead screaming at everyone, I jumped at the opportunity of giving Jim a hand collecting extra medical supplies from the hospital.

The doctor wasn't too happy about handing over his precious bandages, but after a few heated exchanges we managed to get what we wanted, but not wanting to return to the madness of the camp, we took the opportunity to pop in and see Si. We found him on the side of the bed with a pair of pliers and a knife. He was hacking away at his cast, and on seeing us enter the room asked for a hand.

'I'm going with you....I don't give a fuck about my leg....I'm going!'

A quarter of the bottle of whiskey had helped convince Si that a broken leg wouldn't hinder him and he continued to chip away at the cast.

'Come on....help me get it off!'

I looked at Jim who appeared dumbfounded.

'No'

Si looked surprised by our answer and whilst I understood his desire to come; we couldn't ignore his broken leg. Besides, it wasn't his or our choice to make. There was no way the doctor would allow him to go, and what use would he be with a broken leg anyway? But I felt for Si. Not only was he one of the fittest guys in the company, he was also one of the best soldiers and most popular Corporals. I can only imagine how incredibly frustrating it must have been breaking his leg in The Congo, and now having to sit this one out as well. But unfortunately a broken leg is not something you can just 'walk off.' And although we couldn't calm him down, we did eventually manage to get him to except the truth.

By the time we got back, the camp was in predictable chaos and I could hear Cowhead's voice barking out incoherent orders, which always seemed to cause us to run around doing pointless tasks. He seemed to have that ability to make things five times more complicated than they actually were, and so not wanting to get involved I told Jim I was going to track down some batteries for the 'night scope.'

Nipping behind the cook house where I knew it would be quiet, I found Fino sitting on one of the bins having a crafty cigarette. He'd pulled a similar excuse about having to collect something, and joining him for a smoke we engaged in our favourite pastime of complaining about how rubbish some of the Corporals were, and how different we'd be when we were given rank. But after scrounging a cup of coffee from one of the cooks, we decided to make our way back into the melee.

We arrived in Central Africa late the following evening and after spending the night at the airport, headed for the outskirts of Bangui. The climate was different to The Congo, being hotter and less humid. The roads were no wider than dirt tracks and our trucks kicked up clouds of bright red dust which coated everything within seconds. We were heading for a satellite station that transmitted all of the country's telephone calls, and if it was lost to the rebels, then the only way to make contact with the outside world would be via the radios at the airport.

We were spread thinly though and given the number of sites that needed defending around the capital, only our team was being sent to the satellite station. That meant just seven of us including Alf, and if anything kicked off we were about twenty minutes away from the nearest help. On the up side though, Bangui Airport had a permanent French garrison including fighter planes and helicopters, as well as French Army Regulars. Therefore it would be the Legion's job to defend these small outposts, whilst relying on the French Army to keep us supplied. And this situation did get me thinking about the French Government's attitude towards the Legion, because it's a commonly held opinion that the Legion had always been used as 'cannon fodder;' to reduce the risk of any political embarrassment. I don't know that I'm qualified to answer that question in historical terms, but in modern terms I don't think it's that black-and-white. The bulk of the French Army still consisted of national servicemen, and as such the Legion was one of its few professional units. And this, in addition with our ability to deploy at such short notice, meant that we were perfectly suited for such missions....irrespective of any political advantages we might bring.

The satellite station was relatively small, consisting of the satellite itself and two small single-storey buildings, one of which housed all the communications equipment and the other we would use to sleep in. The whole place was surrounded by a ten-foot brick wall and we quickly set up two guard positions. Between the six of us that meant two hours on, four hours off and we were due to stay here for the week. There was also a small detachment of government soldiers who would man the main gate.

Initially I was hacked off at the thought of a solid week of guard duty. Just as in The Congo we wouldn't be allowed to sleep during the day, so that within a couple of days we'd be absolutely knackered; but the thought of being away from the rest of the platoon for seven days made up for it. Although Rocky could have his moments, most of the time he was tolerable....especially when he was away from the other Corporals. Valera had always been fair, and apart from Alf's obvious misgivings he was a good egg. This meant that we always managed to have a laugh and make the most of whatever we were up to, unlike the other two teams in the platoon who had too many arsehole Corporals and Sergeants who constantly made our lives a misery. And so to have a week away from them almost felt like a holiday.

The next few days were a bit of an anticlimax. After The Congo we'd expected to be in the thick of it right from the off, but conflicts in Africa seemed to peter out as quickly as they erupted, and for the moment things appeared quiet. Refugees were still leaving the capital, but the rioting had stopped and for the time being the government had re-established control. This meant that although we kept vigilant, we could at least relax a little and there was even talk of flying back to Gabon within the week. To be honest though most of the team had grown quite found of our little outpost away from everyone else, and for the moment we were happy staying put. We'd even managed to get a deal going with the local village whereby we could get our clothes washed. They had not been washed properly since we'd left Corsica and the local women were prepared to wash a full rucksack for only ten francs. They returned cleaned and pressed and even my rucksack appeared brand new. But probably out of a sense of wanting to alleviate my own guilt, I decided to treble the ten francs to thirty. Not that thirty francs was being over generous, but I just couldn't let someone wash all my clothes by hand for the equivalent of a pound. We'd also managed to bribe the satellite operator into setting up overseas calls for us, and for a small fee I'd managed to phone home. It was wonderful to hear a friendly voice after such a long time, but at the same time it brought sad news. My grandfather had passed away a month earlier and although my mother had contacted the French Embassy, they had refused to pass the news on. I'd been close to my grandfather and remember as a small boy being enthralled by his stories of being a cavalryman serving in India during the 1920's. He'd lived to well into his nineties and although deeply saddened by his death, it was also upsetting to think that he'd been dead for over a month and I hadn't known anything about it. I hated the Legion at times like these. I knew they had an obligation to protect the identity of those who'd taken anonymity, but how hard is it to get a message through to someone like me who wasn't? It just seemed like a ludicrously stupid way to behave.

We all had times when we hated the Legion and I think that's why we appreciated the relative sanity of the satellite station so much. I was coming up to eighteen months' service in the Legion and at times it seemed that most of my service had been spent having orders barked at me. Here, we were away from the bullshit and even Rocky had started to chill out and have a laugh. So the thought of joining the platoon again anytime soon wasn't one that anyone was looking forward to.

Manning the main gate I'd also got the sense that Central Africa was poorer than The Congo. Apart from having fewer tarmac roads, there were a lot of people who didn't have shoes and whose clothes looked like rags. The country didn't seem to have the same infrastructure as The Congo and it was hard to describe, but the people seemed more desperate somehow. The day after we'd had our clothes washed our outpost had been inundated with people wanting to wash our gear. It was sad to have to turn them away, but we just didn't have anything left to wash!

The following day we got away from the satellite station for a few hours after being sent to check on a small missionary outpost that had been set up with donations from western countries. Turning off the main road we headed through a forest and within seconds we were covered in the distinctive red dust. A short while later we passed through a village where our trucks were followed by hordes of screaming children begging for food. They ran after the truck with their arms outstretched until exhaustion finally forced them to give up. We'd been told not to hand out any food, but found it was impossible to refuse them. And when the same thing happened in the next village, we emptied our ration packs as we passed through trying to ensure that everyone got at least something. Admittedly it did turn into a bit of a scrum, but at least it was better than starving. And besides, the fact that these people were prepared to fight over a biscuit spoke volumes about the state of the country.

Nothing though prepared me for the site of the missionary outpost. In my naivety I'd expected a little cluster of small shacks, where the little food that was available was distributed evenly amongst the poor and needy. But not here. This place couldn't be seen behind its ten-foot high pristinely kept white washed walls which contrasted the dirty and dusty villages that lay outside. It sat like an oasis of luxury surrounded by a sea of poverty, and looked more like an exclusive golf club than a missionary outpost. We banged on the thick oak doors and a few minutes later we were confronted by the site of bright green perfectly manicured lawns. Automatic sprinkler systems were busily working away and we were informed that 'Le Patron' was expecting us. The outside world was shut out again and I really didn't know what to think. Newly built chalet style buildings were dotted around the place, each with its own air conditioning unit. And rather than the golf club it now looked more like a holiday complex.

It was hard to believe that on the other side of the wall people were fighting over scraps of food thrown from the back of a truck, whereas this place seemed to be defined by its luxury. Most of the chalets were empty and so we made a bee line towards the sound of a television, where we found some bloke casually supping on a bottle of coke. He was watching what looked like an American game show on a huge ultra-modern TV set, and seeing us standing in the doorway invited us in to join him. It was completely bizarre and I had to pinch myself to accept what my eyes were telling me. But turning away I caught another glimpse of the game show and the penny finally dropped. It wasn't a game show at all. It was one of those religious programmes hosted by someone who just looked like a cheesy game show host. Telephone numbers were running along the bottom of the screen to enable viewers to make donations whilst the perma-tanned game show host gave his sermon. This place it seemed had been constructed from such donations. But rather than building something that might actually benefit the locals and drag them out of poverty, this 'luxury style holiday complex' had been constructed instead.

'Le Patron's' Cartier watch glinted in the sunlight, and taking off his Ray Ban sunglasses he greeted us with a smile that exposed his porcelain white teeth. Asking him whether he was 'all right' seemed a bit daft now, because of cause he was all right. He was probably the most 'all right' person in the whole country. But he nodded anyway with a knowing smile and invited us to stay for lunch. Alf though, to the relief of everyone gave a very curt, but polite, 'No'. I think most of us would have preferred to have sold our souls to the devil rather than sit around the table with this guy. And so, utterly disgusted by the obvious hypocrisy of the place we bade our farewells and left.

It was one of the most unbelievable sights I'd witnessed since being in Africa. And maybe I'd gotten the whole thing wrong. Maybe they were doing great things in the country. But if they were, then they certainly made sure that *they* didn't want for anything.

Our time at the satellite station was drawing to an end and a day later our week was up. We were half expecting to be heading back to the airport and on to Gabon, but instead we headed for a factory that also needed guarding. The country was still unstable and so for the time being our mission hadn't changed. Jim's team had already arrived at the factory but given its size, we'd be joining them. We'd also acquired an extra member of the team whilst at the satellite station and as we drove towards the factory, I could feel him rummaging around inside my combat jacket. Marvin was a mongoose who had befriended us over the past few days and had become a sort of mascot. He was incredibly friendly given their fearsome reputation and because he seemed to live around the satellite station we'd decided to take him with us.

The site of the factory was almost as shocking as the missionary outpost, except this time in a positive way. The factory that we were being sent to guard....this site of strategic importance that could not be allowed to fall into enemy hands under any circumstances....was a Guinness Factory!

It was unimaginable! That here, in the middle of Central Africa which was one of the poorest nations in the world, there was a Guinness Factory. This was the final proof (if proof was needed) that our military commanders didn't have a clue what they were doing. Firstly, how can a Guinness Factory be that important? (Well alright......I'll concede on that point.) And secondly, if it is, the last people you'd send to guard it would be a load of soldiers!

We drove through the main gates and found Jim in his element. Our Irish Corporal was already gulping down a 'pint of the black stuff' and called us over. He was raving about how great this place was and that we'd be here for up to a week. With things pretty quiet in this sector the local government troops hadn't expected us for another day. This meant we had the day off and rather than just sit around we'd decided to throw a party. The drinks situation was obviously taken care of and a couple of the lads were already out sourcing something to eat. The factory boss, who lived on site, had kindly lent us his garden for the event and we were to get ourselves over there straight away.

The beer was already flowing by the time we arrived and it was great to relax with an ice cold pint for the first time in ages. The food situation also improved massively when the lads returned with a live pig they'd bought from a local farmer. With the exception of our two nights in Gabon, we were into our sixth week of ration pack food and our mouths started to water at the thought of a 'hog roast'.

One of the truly unique things in the Legion was the diversity of people who joined, and it was rare if you couldn't find someone who had the right skills when required. Apart from the platoon's obvious translation skills, we also had a Parisian locksmith turned petty thief, who was able to open our barrack doors whenever we lost our keys, a Russian doctor, a Portuguese electrician, a Ukrainian maths teacher, and for this particular situation….a Tahitian butcher. And so whilst he went to work cleaning up the pig, the rest of us set about digging a big hole in the middle of the garden. We lit a huge fire, and once it had burnt down, threw rocks onto the hot embers which we then covered with banana leaves. The pig was then laid on top, covered with a further layer of banana leaves, and the whole thing covered with soil to form a sort of oven.

Four hours later the meat was succulently tender, and washed down with cold beer made for a fantastic feast. It was great to have a night off after so long and although it wasn't exactly a 'nightclub,' it still made all the difference and lifted our moral.

The morning saw a return to the mundane and knackering round of guard duties. Two on, four off was becoming our bible and I couldn't remember the last time I'd had a solid six to eight hours' sleep, but it must have been at least two months ago. It hadn't seemed to matter in The Congo because we were always doing something different and didn't have the time to think about being tired. But here, the monotony and boredom of the guard duties left us too much time to think about little else. And so when Jim asked for help with administering medical treatment to some locals, I jumped at the chance.

He'd agreed to treat a couple of people after patching up one of the factory workers the day before, but nothing had prepared us for the sight that confronted us. Word had spread in the local village that there was a French doctor who was running an open surgery at the factory, and as a result there must have been in excess of fifty people waiting to be treated. The platoon medical kit suddenly looked completely inadequate and there was no way we could deal with these numbers. The only thing we could do was to treat the cuts and open sores, many of which were septic, and send the rest home. It was sad really because many of them were very ill and needed medicines that we just didn't have. There were even a couple of people with malaria who had dragged themselves out of their beds in the hope of receiving treatment. But even so, no one complained at being turned away and the common dignity they showed was humbling.

Heading back, a shot rang out which sent a shiver down my spine and we raced back to see what was going on. Cowhead was in one of the guard positions and on seeing us, told me to bring my sniper rifle. I climbed up to join him and peering out into the surrounding fields, wondered what he was shooting at.

'See that dog?....Shoot it!'

Cowhead was pointing to a dog that was running around the field about 300 metres in front of us. The scum bag had obviously taken a shot and missed and now wanted me to finish it off. It took me a second, but then I realised what he was actually up to. At first I'd thought we were being attacked, but then remembered we'd received orders a couple of days earlier that we should shoot any dogs that looked like they were carrying disease. This hadn't bothered most of the lads, because I'd noticed before how differently a lot of other nationalities viewed dogs. To many of them, they were nothing but dirty scavenging vermin, which completely contradicted our view of dogs being 'man's best friend'. I remember as a five-year-old being brought to tears by my father's bedtime story of 'Bedgellert'. And so although I was prepared to shoot at enemy soldiers, there was no way I was going to shoot some poor dog.

'No I won't....It's too far away to know whether there is anything wrong with it.'

'Are you disobeying an order?'

'OY....COWHEAD!'

Jim had been listening to us. And apart from being a medic he was obviously a bit of a dog lover.

'You shoot that dog....and I will fucking shoot you!'

There was that look of complete seriousness on Jim's face which was never usually present, and he unslung his rifle as if to emphasise his point. He was normally a pretty placid kind of a bloke and his outburst had taken Cowhead by surprise, and he appeared even more confused than he normally was. He opened his mouth a few times as if he was about to say something, but nothing came out, and in the end pushed past me and climbed down from the guard position, heading off in the direction of the rest of the platoon and complaining that he was only following orders.

I don't know whether Jim would have shot him or not. Most probably he wouldn't have done. But then that's easy to say when it's not me he's threatening to shoot.

It was bizarre really how worked up we got about it. We'd grown used to seeing cruelty dished out to our fellow Legionnaires, but seeing it directed towards a dog had sparked something inside. Maybe it was because it seemed so helpless, or maybe there was just something about dogs that was deeply embedded in our national psyche, which we could never explain and that people like Cowhead could never understand. Either way, it seemed like a cause worthy of getting worked up about. And getting one over on Cowhead was always worth the effort.

A week later we were back at the airport and waiting to fly back to Gabon. It had been a strange time in Central Africa, and although I'd spent most of it bored out of my skull on guard, it had also been incredibly interesting at the same time. It might not have been the 'gung ho fest' we'd been led to believe, but the peace and calm had enabled me to take a closer look at the country, and that was something that even in The Congo we'd not really been able to do. The Central Africans I'd met had seemed dignified and gracious, determined to make something of their lives and not allowing themselves to be dissuaded by the obvious disadvantages of living in one of the poorest countries in the world. I don't know whether the democratically elected government was actually democratic or not, or whether they were just being held to ransom by the world banks, but it appeared to me that there was something incredibly wrong with a country that had mineral reserves including oil, diamonds and uranium, and yet still couldn't afford to pay its soldiers and left its civilians short of food.

I was glad to be leaving Central Africa....not least because I needed a break and a good night's sleep. Our four month tour of Gabon was almost half over and so far we'd spent no more than a few days there. Maybe when we touched down this time, we might actually start the jungle course.

Jungle School

Gabon's capital Libreville seemed incredibly cosmopolitan compared with The Congo and Central Africa. It stretched along the coastline, making the most of the beautiful golden beaches that in other parts of the world would have tourists flocking to them in their thousands. Here though, they appeared mostly deserted, apart from a couple of lone fishermen who seemed to have the whole Atlantic Ocean to fish from.

Our fifteen-minute taxi ride into town took us past the Central Business District and modern high rise hotels. The country had prospered through exploiting its oil reserves, and its political stability had made it one of the wealthiest countries in the region. The French Army had remained in Gabon after its independence from France in 1960 and its troops were permanently rotated on four month tours. For Legionnaires it was classed as the 'peach' tour, providing both excellent jungle training facilities and a superb nightlife. It was the latter that we were about to experience and for most of us it would be our first taste of freedom in months. Unlike Calvi, Libreville provided an opportunity to enjoy a drink out of the glare of the Military Police, and after The Congo and Central Africa we couldn't wait.

Our first stop was a restaurant, and the manager welcomed us with open arms as we entered. We obviously had a reputation for being big payers because most restaurants would have been making excuses about being fully booked at the sight of a group of half-cut soldiers. But the manager, who looked like a bingo caller in his tasteful sequinned jacket showed us to what he called, 'the best table in the house'.

'Hey….look at Hugh Hefner over there!'

Tom had spotted Fino, who was sitting at the other 'best table in the house.' He had befriended a couple of local girls, who were draping themselves all over him, and he was entertaining them with the help of a couple of bottles of champagne. Puffing away on a huge Cuban cigar, he noticed us enter and casually waved at us, acknowledging our presence like some kind of Italian Mafia boss. I'm sure that anyone else would have thought he owned the place as the waiters ran round after him. Obviously they didn't sell too many bottles of champagne and didn't want to lose his custom, because the one thing that they could always guarantee was that we would pay. After all, they knew where we lived and any complaint would normally result in us being restricted to barracks. That meant we'd happily give the shirts off our backs before deciding not to pay or causing trouble.

We tucked into a huge plate of steak and washed it down with a load more beer before leaving Fino, who had just ordered another bottle of Champagne, and heading for the towns' main night spot. The trouble was that it was full of Legionnaires, and more depressingly, Corporals and Sergeants. The last thing we wanted was to drink in a place surrounded by the exact people we'd come to get away from. But there didn't seem anywhere else to go, until Jim suggested a bar he knew from his previous tour of Gabon. The bar was called 'Chez Tantine' but it was off limits to all Legionnaires.

Our barracks were situated on the outskirts of town and the rules for going out were simple. Go out of the main gate and go straight on. Do not ever go out of the main gate and turn right.

Turning right was forbidden, because within ten minutes walk you'd find yourself in one of the city's poorest slums, a sprawling collection of hand-built shacks constructed from corrugated iron and old bits of wood. Open sewers ran down the middle of the roads and the place was a maze of unlit alleys and narrow passageways.

This was where Gabon's underclass lived and unfortunately for us was also where Chez Tantines was. We knew that four-half cut Legionnaires with money in their pockets would make a prime target, but unable to face Cowhead and his cronies any longer, we decided to take the chance.

The cocktail of beer and bravado must have stopped us worrying because we were in high spirits as we sped back in the direction of Tantine. Someone mentioned taxi surfing, and giving the driver some money not to pull over we took it in turns to climb out of the back window and onto the roof of the car. The beer might have steadied my nerves but did nothing for my balance, but even so it felt exhilarating and intoxicating to be standing on the roof as we sped along the coastline. And Tom, who was always the comedian, had us in stitches when he leaned over and knocked on the outside of the front windscreen, almost giving the taxi driver a heart attack.

We crouched down in the seats as the taxi drove past the font of the barracks and two minutes later we stopped at the edge of the township, the driver refusing to go any further. We set off up the main street like we were on patrol. Jim and Tom were at the head of our box formation with myself and Si at the back. We kept to the centre of the road, which would give us time to react to anyone coming out of the hidden alleyways, and made our way cautiously down the main road. There was complete silence apart from the odd barking dog in the distance, but I could feel a thousand eyes watching our every step. I was hoping Jim had not forgotten the way, and was beginning to loose faith when he stopped next to a couple of large corrugated iron gates. He banged on the doors which echoed around the streets causing more dogs to start barking before he was answered by a little old woman. She must have been seventy if she was a day, and after a brief pause to focus on us in the dim light her face broke into a huge toothless smile.

'JIMMY!.....my friend....welcome....come in!'

This then was Tantine herself, and this place was hers. Whilst in here we knew we were safe. No one ever messed with Tantine in her own bar, but once outside we were on our own.

The courtyard led to a bar that was no more than a shack, dimly lit with coloured lights. Bits of old lino covered the dirt floor and a battered stereo was playing in the corner. It might not have been exactly sophisticated, but it did have character and was incredibly atmospheric. We sat down and ordered a drink and I suddenly realised what the overriding allure of this place was. For the first time in the eighteen months since joining the Legion I felt relaxed. Not just sitting in a bar with a beer relaxed, but completely and utterly at ease. Everywhere else there was always the shadow of the regiment that followed you wherever you went. It was always present in the barracks, and even back in Calvi the military police roamed the streets and bars telling you to put your Kepi on straight or smarten yourself up. And even if they weren't, the bars were always full of some of the idiots you were trying to get away from. It was impossible to escape and meant that you always relaxed with one eye looking over your shoulder. But here, for the first time ever we didn't feel that presence at all. Here we could just relax and enjoy ourselves without wondering whether some arsehole was going to come in and start gobbing off. Here, in this dilapidated old shack, run by an old lady and frequented by the odd local, we had finally found somewhere to call our own.

We drank well into the night before Si's antics convinced us it was time to leave. Earlier on in the evening he'd decided to bite into a cactus plant that was sitting on the bar and had reacted to the poison. His lips had swelled to three times their normal size and he looked like he'd just had collagen implants. He looked absolutely ridiculous and it was impossible to look at him without laughing. But he'd continued drinking and after a few too many whiskeys decided to bite into a glass. He was just sitting there at the bar and then without warning, simply put the glass to his mouth and took a chunk out of it. His mouth starting pouring with blood as he spat the bits of glass back out onto the bar. We grabbed him and made sure there were no bits left before making our apologies to Tantine and leaving. She seemed unfazed by the whole thing and just told us to keep an eye out on our way home.

Our military patrol was now more of a stagger as we meandered down the road trying to find our way out of the township. Si was having trouble walking and we had to keep stopping to push him in the right direction, but it was Tom who spotted the car coming up the road.

I don't know why, but we new that there was never any question that this was trouble, and my adrenaline instantly started to sober me up. We fell back into a line on the side of the road and picked up anything that came to hand to face off the four blokes that got out of the car. Two were armed with machetes and started shouting whilst making their way towards us. The good thing about the township was that there were bits of discarded metal everywhere, and I armed myself with an old piece of piping that was lying on the floor. With nowhere to run, we had no choice but to stand our ground and see what transpired. Si was already waving a plank of wood above his head and seemed to be looking forward to a fight. But not dissuaded by his shouting, they broke into a sprint and came straight for us. I focused on the guy in front of me and somehow managed to deflect a swipe from his machete. He swung again, and again I managed to block it with the steel pipe before kicking him in the bollocks causing him to stagger back. He looked up and was about to come at me again when Si's plank caught him on the side of the head. It was followed up with a boot that finished him off and looking round, Tom already had one of the blokes on the ground. He was busy punching the living daylights out of him and didn't seem to have any intention of stopping until Jim shouted out:

'RUN!....COME ON!....LETS GO!'

Jim's sword fighting skills had obviously been more advanced than mine, because he'd seen off the other machete guy with a couple of well placed strikes. (He later told me that all those fights he'd had with 'hurling' sticks whilst playing for the school team had finally come in handy.) We sprinted to the edge of the township into the safety of the main road, lit by street lamps, that ran around the back of the barracks, before scaling the back wall undetected and finally making it back to our rooms.

'APPEL!....APPEL!'

One thing that I certainly didn't miss whilst being in The Congo or Central Africa was *appel*, but back in barracks we'd returned to the old routine. Gabon's working regime was different though to Calvi due to the afternoon heat. The working day here started at 6.30 which meant that appel was at 5.30, but even being an hour earlier than normal, my body still automatically switched to auto-pilot on hearing those words.

I put my sports clothes on and headed towards the door, tripping over a stool. Jim was still snoring heavily and I kicked the end of his bed to hurry him along. Marvin (our mongoose mascot that we'd brought back to Gabon) was asleep on Jim's head and he looked like he was wearing a 'Davy Crocket' hat, but he groaned and eventually started to move. We'd only been in bed a couple of hours after our night out and we weren't the only ones feeling a bit rough. Appel is normally quite a formal affair with the whole platoon paraded in front of the duty Sergeant who is handed a 'slip' by the duty Corporal. The 'slip' is filled in with the whereabouts of everyone in the platoon; i.e. so many in the hospital, so many on guard, so many present, etc. Once all of the platoon's slips have been collated, they are then passed up the chain of command; and because Appel is held twice a day, this means that there is always a precise record of the location of every single Legionnaire.

We paraded outside as we normally would have and sprang to attention when the duty Sergeant stood in front of us. The plan now was to get ourselves dismissed as soon as possible and get back upstairs and try and sober up within the next hour. But the Sergeant took his time reading the 'slip,' before looking up and addressing the duty Corporal.

'Just two things Corporal before you get yourselves away....

Firstly....this slip is completely blank

Oh....and secondly....you're not wearing any pants!....or any shoes!....or any socks!'

The rest of the platoon was still so drunk that no one had noticed the Corporal's lack of clothing and we burst out laughing. Under any other circumstances the Corporal would have been in jail. But given that this was our first night out after the Congo and Central Africa, the Sergeant must have taken pity on him and decided to see the funny side. He dismissed us with a smirk and we scurried away in search of a strong coffee and a cold shower.

The next few days were taken up with the inevitable round of cleaning jobs, which as ever, consisted of the Corporals and Sergeants sitting around smoking and gobbing off whilst the rest of us sweated buckets. But at least the boredom was finally broken when we were told that we'd be jumping the next day.

Most of us hadn't jumped in months and so I was a feeling slightly nervous standing on the runway doing up my parachute. The worst thing that could happen now would be to be pulled out of line by the jump master for incorrectly fastening my chute. And because it had been a while I was just hoping that I hadn't forgotten anything. Fortunately I didn't, but one of the Legionnaires from another platoon did, and as punishment spent most of the night scrubbing. (Embarrassing your platoon in front of the whole company is never a good idea.) I still had a few butterflies as the plane took off but within a few minutes they had disappeared and I couldn't wait to get out. Laden down with our gear and squeezed into the seats, the inside of the plane was like an oven. When we'd flown to The Congo the pilots had lowered the tailgate slightly to allow some air in, but the temperatures in Gabon seemed to be getting hotter by the day as we neared the rainy season. All we could do was to keep as still as possible and make the most of the stuffy air.

A cheer went up when the side doors opened and a blast of cold air shot down the aircraft. Fortunately I was in the first stick and a few minutes later found myself floating gently down to earth under a brilliantly hot sun. The DZ in Gabon was a small sand bar that sat about a mile off the coast and could only be reached by boat. It was like landing on cotton wool and after handing in my parachute there was nothing left to do except sit on the beach. The whole jump had been run by the French Army and was one of the most relaxing ever. And with the plane having to return for more paratroopers before we could be picked up, we spent most of the morning sunning ourselves of the beach. It was fantastic because back at Calvi the DZ was like concrete in places and no sooner had we landed, we'd be up in the air again....No wonder Gabon was such a favourite tour.

The parachute jump had got me fired up for the jungle course and I couldn't wait to get stuck into the training. The Jungle Commando School was run by the French Army and the programme consisted of four weeks' training and a final week-long exercise to test everything we'd learnt. Not only would the school teach us the obvious stuff like map reading techniques, tactics and how to live in the jungle, but we'd also be learning how to survive. Like the different foods that could be eaten and the life-saving medicines to be found, if only you knew where to look. We'd also be put through the five-hour long assault course that was located in the swamplands. The record was held by the regiment and it was considered disrespectful if we didn't get at least somewhere near the fastest time. I'd also be losing the sniper rifle and replacing it with a FAMAS that was much more suitable for the jungle.

The dampness of the morning air had caused a slight mist to settle on the ground and the first rays of light were already penetrating the jungle canopy. I zipped back the mosquito net that was built into my hammock and looked out into the rainforest. Fino already had a brew on, and on seeing me pointed towards Alf who was still asleep. We both started to laugh as quietly as possible when we remembered the drama from the previous night. There had been a tremendous crash followed by shouting and groaning when Alf's hammock had suddenly collapsed. In the pitch black he'd dropped three feet onto a large tree root, but his groaning had only been met by laughter as people woke up and realised what had happened. He then started complaining about the strength of the cord we'd been issued to suspend our hammocks with, until finally giving up and sleeping on the floor. With the camp starting to come to life I pulled on my wet combats which felt slimy and damp. Like many armies we worked with a wet and dry set of clothing. The wet set was always worn during the day because even just moving around in the jungle would be enough to drench you in sweat. This meant that attempting to keep dry during the day was pretty much impossible and so the theory was to not bother trying. This way we had dry clothing to wear during the evening and could avoid foot rot and any other conditions brought about by being permanently damp.

The platoon had been split into its three teams and was being taught the finer points of how to navigate in the jungle, which would test even the most competent map reader. Under normal circumstances the fundamentals of map reading are quite easy. Whether you're trekking in the mountains or on a 'city break', the basic principle is to simply identify features you can see and look for them on the map. A compass can then help orientate the map and give you your exact location. But in the jungle these basic principles are much more difficult to follow. The landscape will change with the seasons, and trails or footpaths that hadn't been used in a couple of months would be reclaimed by the jungle, hiding any evidence of their existence. It was also impossible to see most features anyway because the jungle was so dense in places that visibility could be down to only a few metres. But there are a number of methods to navigate by, one of which is to walk in a dead straight line following a compass bearing. If we could also calculate how far we had walked, then in theory we should know exactly where we were.

Alf's nose was twitching like mad as he halted us for the fifth time in ten minutes. We'd been walking around the jungle for the last couple of hours and I was drenched in sweat. I took another swig from my water bottle and sat down on the trunk of a fallen tree. I could hear monkeys jumping around high up in the canopy. I couldn't see anything through the tangle of vines and thick foliage, but I was beginning to really enjoy the whole simplicity of the jungle. Much greater emphasis was being placed on the basics of survival and it was obvious that combat techniques had hardly changed in over half a century. Being able to just survive in the jungle was half the battle, and this uncomplicated approach to soldiering was appealing.

It was obvious we were lost because Alf had already disregarded Ducs', Fino's and Valera's compasses as being faulty because none of them matched up with his map. Anyone else might start to question the map reading but Alf was convinced that all the compasses were wrong and ploughed on regardless. He was becoming more and more irate and eventually blew his top and started kicking hell out of a termite mound. We were already well overdue for an exercise that should have taken no more than an hour, and the rest of the platoon would already be busy setting up camp, whilst we were still hacking our way through the jungle. The bamboo shoots looked like scaffolding poles sticking out of the ground and took forever to hack through with our machetes. With my hands blistering Alf was now beginning to piss everyone off, but he eventually accepted Valera's offer to take a look at the map. After a careful consultation we moved off in yet another direction.

Valera had not wanted to embarrass Alf anymore than he was already doing himself, but he later told us that Alf had been going in exactly the wrong direction. Instead of heading due West, we'd been going due East!! He had actually held the map the wrong way up and moved off. It was about as basic a mistake as it was possible to make. The one thing that had always been drummed into us, even back at 'The Farm,' was to orientate the map before you did anything else. I liked Alf, but at times his incompetence was absolutely infuriating, and we hacked our way out of the jungle in disgust. When we eventually returned to the bivouac site, we were greeted with jeers by the rest of the platoon who had already set up their hammocks and changed into their dry clothing. But as ever in the Legion, having a team commander like Alf came as a mixed blessing. Ten minutes after arriving back and whilst we busied ourselves with our hammocks, Cowhead had the rest of the platoon doing press-ups as punishment for not doing something to his satisfaction. He was a complete imbecile and I would much prefer to hack my way around the jungle with Alf than have to listen to him barking orders at me.

In an hour or so it would be pitch black and almost impossible to see your hand in front of your face, which made moving in the jungle at night impossible. Bedding down I noticed Alf had dispensed with the idea of setting his hammock up in the trees and had simply laid it on the floor. And with only the odd candle light penetrating the inky blackness, the jungle started to come alive.

Night time was when much of the wildlife ventured out in search of food, and the constant noise of movement only a few feet away was quite unnerving at first. But on another level it was incredibly rewarding to be learning how to survive in such an environment. It had quickly become apparent that a machete was by far the most important piece of our survival kit, and a candle came a close second. I hadn't realised just how black it got in the jungle and just how long it stayed dark for. A torch would soon run out of batteries whereas the candle could last you for weeks. But with the sound of the crickets droning in my ears I could feel myself beginning to fall asleep, when what sounded like a small log bounced off my waterproof bash and landed on the floor with a thud. I could hear rustling in the trees and just presumed it must be a dead branch that had come loose, but within seconds it felt like the whole tree was going to come down as it shook violently. The monkeys' harrowing, deathly screams shattered the darkness and branches started to fall like raindrops. I took cover and put my hands over my head, helpless to do anything else. You could hear branches being shaken and snapped as the monkeys went on the rampage. Alf was shouting out something obvious like 'Don't Move....Take Cover' (evidently concerned about anyone who was out taking a midnight stroll.) Birds and other forms of wildlife joined in with the commotion and the air exploded into a barrage of screeches.

The bombardment of branches seemed to last for ages but was probably over in no more than a few minutes, and as quickly as it had started, the jungle soon returned once again to a state of peaceful harmony. I had no idea whether we were being targeted, or if the monkeys were running from something, or whether they were simply out hunting. But it was one of the most unexpected experiences ever. And as it happened, it could not have been a more apt introduction to 'booby traps' and ambushes, which was the next lesson we were about to learn.

There must be an old military doctrine which states that soldiers will listen more attentively if they are run ragged before any lesson, but we easily kept up with the jungle instructor as he sprinted along the narrow jungle trails. I was even beginning to quite enjoy myself when Ducs, who was at the front of our group, suddenly disappeared. He'd fallen into a 'bear pit' which the instructor had carefully side-stepped at the last minute, and we gathered around to look in. The pit was probably four or five feet deep and Ducs was lying at the bottom groaning. Apart from having the wind knocked out of him he seemed fine and after a few minutes of us taking the piss, he started to climb out. The instructors had obviously used this trick a thousand times before and I'm sure that it never failed, and it definitely demonstrated to us just how suitable the jungle environment was for booby traps. In a western environment digging a bear pit in the middle of an existing footpath and trying to camouflage it would be almost impossible. But due to the closeness of the foliage and the amount of dead leaves that were on the floor anyway, in the jungle it was relatively simple. Almost too simple really, because with half a dozen sharpened pieces of bamboo dug into the pit, Ducs would have ended up looking like a tea bag. But in a way, that really summed up what booby traps were all about. Arguably the effort needed to dig the pit wasn't worth it, if it could only kill or injure a single soldier. But the psychological effect on the rest of the soldiers seeing one of their mates mutilated in such a gruesome way would be devastating. If done properly then, a number of carefully placed booby traps could have a whole regiment tiptoeing around the jungle for weeks. During the Vietnam War, some companies of American Infantry stated that 100% of their casualties were due to enemy booby traps, and that the effect of having to fight this invisible enemy was reducing their combat effectiveness.

We spent the next couple of days perfecting our booby trap making skills and learning where best to place them to have maximum effect. Apart from the 'bear pit' there were smaller traps that would use the weight of the victim to push spikes into the lower leg. As the victim stood on the trap, it would give way and bamboo spikes positioned like a set of pliers, would skewer the leg, and the more the victim pushed the more they tightened. But there were also elaborately constructed traps like the innocently named 'Brosse a Dente', or 'toothbrush'. This consisted of a number of sharpened wood sticks that were lashed horizontally to one end of a six-foot piece of wood, so that I suppose it did vaguely resemble a toothbrush. It would then be set at just above knee height with the main shaft pulled right back. Once released by a trip wire it would spring forward with such force that the spikes would pass straight through the victim's legs, leaving him physically attached to the 'toothbrush.' But the most elaborate and deadly of all was the 'Wrecking Ball.' This was a spiked ball made out of pieces of sharpened bamboo and about the same size as a space hopper. It was then hung on the end of a ten metre cord or vine and hoisted into the tree line. Once sprung it would swing silently like a giant pendulum increasing in speed and could easily take out of couple of victims. It would then swing back for another go, hitting anyone who hadn't taken cover. We set one up and it was devastating enough just watching it flail around the jungle like a steel construction ball. But we were also taught more basic traps, like wedging a grenade that's had its pin removed under a tree root and attaching a simple trip wire. This could be set up in seconds and would considerably slow down any pursuing enemy force. And we even had a trip wire attached to a FAMAS that was wedged into a tree. It would fire off a magazine on full auto and hopefully kill or injure the enemy, but it would also give the impression that they were being ambushed by a group of soldiers. They may later find the FAMAS and realise the truth or they may not. But it all added to the psychological and morale-draining effect of a well placed booby trap. They could put the enemy on the back foot and drain his fighting spirit.

It was an incredibly interesting couple of days, if being rather macabre at times. But we were soon back with Alf who was now teaching us the finer points of how to make an improvised parachute from a standard issue waterproof poncho. This though was more than just a lesson. During the final exercise we had to navigate our way to a jungle clearing and radio for our supplies to be brought in by helicopter. The scenario would be that it was impossible to land, and so our food would be dropped by the parachute we were now making.

Alf had watched a brief demonstration and was now ordering us about. But by the time we'd finished it didn't look anything like the instructors' example. Alf had obviously misunderstood some vital piece of information and Valera started sighing dejectedly. But we were running out of time and so we gave our feeble effort to Fino, who as a trained parachute packer, could at least ensure that it deployed properly if nothing else. As it stood then, it looked like we were going hungry on the final exercise. But that was still a couple of weeks away and for the time being we had more pressing concerns.

We loaded into the trucks and made our way down to the coast and the swamplands where the assault course was located. It would be run as a platoon and would take us anywhere between four and six hours to complete. The company Commander had turned up and was expecting a good performance. Obviously the kudos of being able to brag about holding the assault course record back in the officers' mess would be unsurpassed, and he was busy handing out encouragement about representing the company and the regiment etc. But that was the first time for me, and probably everyone else, we'd ever received encouraged in the Legion. Most of the time nothing was ever said, but it was always expected that we gave 120%, because we knew the consequences if we didn't. The most that ever happened would be someone threatening to beat us to a pulp if we didn't win, and so the Captain's words were immediately met with suspicion. However, for probably the only time in his life, Cowhead came into his own, and rescued the situation by promising to drown in the swamp anyone who he deemed not to be putting in enough effort....And so with the equilibrium in the platoon restored, we set off.

Within minutes we were swimming through dirty brown water and I was suddenly grateful to my parents who had taught me to swim at such an early age. As a result I was now a fairly strong swimmer and if ever I needed to be, it was here. We were weighed down with a small rucksack and an old sub machine gun from the 1950's that no longer worked. We also had concrete-filled ammunition boxes that had to be carried between us, and within minutes

I was knackered. When we could touch the bottom, the roots were so thick that they kept tripping us up and we would disappear underwater, only to re-surface a few seconds later with a mouthful of swamp water. The rucksack also acted like a dead weight dragging you under and a few of the weaker swimmers kept disappearing and had to be helped along. After twenty minutes we reached the first obstacle. It was a twelve-foot high piece of wooden sheeting that was angled at forty-five degrees and completely smooth. It was impossible to climb and we had to form a human pyramid to make our way to the top. It was incredibly hard work and we still had at least four hours to go.

The riverbeds gave way to bogs which were five feet deep in places. Pulling myself through felt like I was dragging a tractor and the only way to make it was to keep the momentum going. Stopping would see you sink up to your neck in the thick mud and once stuck it would be impossible to get going again. I was pushing myself forward with everything I had and still it must have looked like I was walking in slow motion. Fino, who had already broken through onto dry land, threw his jacket back for me to grab hold of, and with a final effort, I popped out and landed in a heap covered in mud.

The assault course continued and included everything from individual obstacles, to having to improvise a stretcher and carry one of the lads over a series of obstacles. It was absolutely knackering and we finally finished in five hours twenty minutes. A fast time we were told, but still a little way off the record. But the Captain seemed pleased enough, and so dead on our feet, we trudged our way back to the bivouac site. Freshly caught fish had been laid on, and in no time at all we'd constructed a raised grilling rack out of bamboo, and cooked the fish using the heat from the smoke.

We spent the next couple of weeks in and out of the jungle, splitting our time between the normal garrison duties in Libreville and the commando course. We would spend day after day perfecting patrolling tactics in the jungle and setting up snap ambushes. It was incredibly tiring both physically and mentally. You had to stay alert all the time and react in the correct way whether that was being ambushed by an enemy or being involved in a company attack. Live firing exercises were crucial to the training and we would expend tens of thousands of rounds. It was a completely new kind of warfare, where most of the fire fights would be conducted at extremely close quarters. The FAMAS, with its three-round burst capability was ideal for this type of fighting and we would spend hours repeating the exact same drills until they were perfect.

We also spent a week further down the coast at a place called Port Gentil and had a superb couple days at the ranges with the group of French Special Forces, where we fired everything from shotguns to heavy calibre half-inch sniper rifles. It was great fun and as there was no official firing range, we simply stuck a couple of targets in the sand by the water's edge and fired out to sea.

But on 1st September something happened that took me by complete surprise. We were sitting in the guard room when Ducs came in and told us that Princess Diana had been killed in a car crash in Paris the day before. And to my complete surprise, Brunescu immediately ordered a two-minute silence in her honour. I couldn't believe that here….in a guard room in Gabon that French Foreign Legionnaires were holding a two-minutes silence in honour of Princess Diana. I knew that she was popular back home, but I had no idea that she had this much appeal abroad. Brunescu seemed physically upset and for a moment I felt guilty that I wasn't as saddened as he was. He even came over afterwards and tapped me on the shoulder as if I'd just lost a close personal friend. The whole episode was just bizarre. But I suppose it's one of those moments in history where people say that everyone can remember exactly where they were when they heard the news. And with a two-minute silence, I could hardly forget.

But a week later I found myself standing in the door of a Transal, looking out onto the thick Gabonese jungle. My canopy opened, bringing me to a standstill in the air and I looked around to try and get my bearings. The cool air felt refreshing after being stuck in the plane for the last hour and I breathed in a huge lungful.

The drop zone had been cut out of the forest and although we had never used it before, its distinctive rectangle shape was easy to make out. I pulled the Velcro handle on my front and my rucksack slid off my legs and was left dangling six metres below me from a cord attached to my harness. I had packed my water bottles in the middle of the rucksack and just hoped they wouldn't burst on impact. But with the ground getting closer I waited until I felt the rucksack cord slacken. This meant that my rucksack had landed and gave me a two-second warning. I braced myself for the impact and landed mercifully without injury. We had a three-day march through the jungle ahead of us and I didn't want to start off with a twisted ankle.

Our regrouping point was a small hill at the southern end of the drop zone and so after folding my parachute up and placing it on top of my rucksack, I quickly checked my compass and set off. It might sound a little over-cautious to check my compass, but landing in the middle of an unfamiliar area can be incredibly disorientating. And with Legionnaires running in all directions towards their respective regrouping points, those first few minutes can be unbelievably confusing.

Dumping my kit down on the floor, I set up in a defensive position whilst the rest of the platoon slowly made their way in until Alf was the only one still missing. The Adjutant had the Captain on the radio asking if we were all in place, and so he asked if anyone had seen Alf. Someone shouted out they'd seen him packing his chute away. Which immediately begged the question that if he wasn't injured, then where was he? But with the Captain putting pressure on the platoon to get moving, the Adjutant appointed Valera as our new team commander. We couldn't wait any longer and Alf would have to sort himself out. But as we set off Fino spotted a lone figure about 600 metres away heading our way. It was difficult to make out at first but it soon become clear that it was the unmistakable figure of Alf. He was running as fast as he could and on reaching our position, collapsed in a heap. He'd run the full length of the DZ carrying his rucksack, parachute, reserve parachute and wearing a steel helmet in the midday jungle heat. His olive green combat jacket had turned dark green with sweat which was also dripping in huge droplets from his protruding nose. It was a tremendous feat of physical stamina, especially right before the march. And although Alf might have difficulty telling the difference between north and south, at times like this I couldn't help but have a huge admiration for the bloke's sheer determination and spirit.

We set off into the jungle and immediately started to make slow progress. The undergrowth was like barbed wire and after three hours' hard labour we'd only covered just over a kilometre, but with the light beginning to fade we set up our camp for the night. We each had a single twenty-four hour ration pack and the rest of our food would be made up of what we could forage from the jungle and whatever the helicopter dropped. The ration packs consisted of two main meals that had to be eaten once opened and so as a precaution I buddied up with Fino. We shared a meal between us and at least this way our half rations would last us two days. We'd been taught how to find food in the jungle, but it was a skill that required a lot more than a few days' training to master, and as for setting traps, we simply didn't have the time. And so after a few spoonfuls of meat and carrots each, we flipped a coin to see who would lick the tin out.

The next morning we made better time by following some existing trails. But it was equally hard going as we spent most of the time either climbing up or scrambling down the steep muddy slopes. A gargantuan effort only saw us manage to walk five kilometres all day, but if that wasn't depressing enough, then the sight of our food plummeting to earth was the final nail in the coffin. The other two teams in the platoon watched as their homemade parachute opened perfectly and fluttered gently to earth, revealing a small but adequate amount of rice. Ours on the other hand, after a promising start, broke away from the poncho and fell like a lead weight exploding on impact and sending rice everywhere. Practically all of it was ruined ending up in a muddy field, but as if to rub salt into the wound, a bottle of Soya source did manage to survive. Utterly hacked off we set up our camp and watched the rest of the platoon tucking into half a mug of rice each. But just as it was getting dusk we heard a call for help from Valera. He'd nipped off into the jungle to take a dump and his call for help was in fact more of a shriek than a call. You could sense the terror in his voice and we sprinted to see what was causing him such alarm.

It was almost with a sense of trepidation that we pulled back the foliage, not quite sure what we were going to find. But there, with his pants still around his ankles was Valera. He had his foot pressed down hard onto the head of a ten-foot python, stopping it from moving. Sensing it was trapped it was starting to wrap its body around Valera's leg and you could see the fear etched into his face. He was frozen to the spot and started shouting for help. Alf was right behind us and came charging through the undergrowth, tripping up on a root and landing on the floor.

'What's wrong....What's wrong....SHIT....OH MY GOD.... Don't move I'll get it off....'

He drew his machete which caused Valera to panic even more. If Alf's machete skills were anything like his map reading then Valera would be missing a foot shortly.

'NO don't....You'll miss....!'

'No I won't....Just don't move....'

'AHHHHHHHHHHHHHHH!!'

'It's dead....It's dead....Calm down!'

It wasn't exactly the cleanest of kills. In fact the first couple of blows seemed to piss the snake off, but eventually it was slain and slowly released its hold on Valera, who, apart from his pride was fortunately not injured. But he had also inadvertently gone some way to solving the food issue. With the Soya source the meat might just be edible and over an open fire we cooked some of the snake. I couldn't honestly say that it was tasty, but if you swallowed it without chewing too much it was just about palatable.

The following morning we dropped our hammocks for the final time and set off towards our final destination. The going was tough at first, but after negotiating our way through a couple of swamps, the ground became firmer and the jungle less claustrophobic as we got nearer to the coast, and on the edge of a clearing we stopped for lunch. (For our team that meant a drink of water and a cigarette.) The landscape of the clearing looked like it had been lifted straight out of a scene from *The Land That Time Forgot*. The grass was lush and green and the whole area was pockmarked like a First World War battlefield, so that you walked from one small crater directly into the next. There were giant toadstool shapes dotted everywhere which were constructed out of mud. Presumably they must have been anthills at one time and had since been baked hard in the sun.

I gulped down the water and was busy squashing a big red ant that was crawling up my neck when we all heard what sounded like something crashing through the jungle. During the day the jungle was reasonably quiet, but this was deafening and sounded like the whole forest was being uprooted. Whatever it was it was huge and was getting louder.

'ELEPHANTS!....Move into the clearing'

Elephants! Since when have elephants lived in the jungle? We grabbed our gear and headed into the clearing as the sound grew louder and louder until we could see branches swaying in front of us. I tried hard to see through the dense jungle screen but could only hear as the great beasts demolished everything in their path. Trees could be heard snapping and the devastation sounded colossal, but the thickness of the jungle restricted our view to a few shadowy shapes. They never broke into the clearing and within a few minutes had passed us by. The jungle looked like it had been flattened by a bulldozer, but the guilty culprits' huge footprints that were everywhere were already filling up with water. No doubt within a matter of weeks the jungle would be back to new and ready for the next herd.

We continued on our way hacking through the jungle until we suddenly popped out onto a sandy beach. There in front of us was the Atlantic Ocean, and leaving our stuff on the sand we cooled off in its refreshing waters. The beach was lined with coconut tress and was littered with their fruits that sat untouched in the sand. Not having eaten properly in three days we set about trying to open them up, but it was incredibly hard work and soon became a mammoth job. Even with a machete, pulling off the thick husk was like trying to peel back strips of sheet metal. And frustration had already gotten the better of Ducs, who was futilely throwing one against a rock. But after twenty minutes of exhaustive work it finally gave up its prize and tasted amazing.

The jungle course was now over and an hour later we boarded a chopper for the trip back to Libreville. It had been a superb time and one I'd thoroughly enjoyed. Most soldiers say that the jungle environment in like Marmite. You either love it or hate it. And I can honestly say that you can keep your snow covered mountains and give me the jungle any day of the week.

Home Run

With only a few weeks left to the tour, we started on the 'big clean up' of the barracks in preparation for the next regiment that was taking over. And when we weren't cleaning, we were packing stuff into boxes. Everything had to checked, rechecked, checked again and then sealed into wooden crates. It was frustratingly bureaucratic but at the same time typically French. And with the Legion's work ethic thrown into the mix, where only the Legionnaires worked whilst the other half of the company sat around lording it, what should have taken a couple of days ended up taking well over a week. But we did have a huge motivation to work and one that occupied our every thought. We had been promised leave on our return from Gabon, and that single thought was enough to make any level of work tolerable. But with the Legion still holding our passports, the official line was that we had to stay in France.

Not that this rule stopped most of us from trying, and since the formation of the European Union, not having a passport was not as restrictive as you might think. For the Brits it was relatively straightforward. Simply turn up at the airport or the port and buy a ticket with your Military ID Card. As an official form of ID it could now be used to travel between countries within the European Union. But that said you still had to be careful. If the airline ticketing officials wanted to get all 'Big Brother' on you and call the Gendarmerie over, then leave would be spent in jail. It was a gamble, but with the chance of getting home being dangled in front of you it was one that most people thought was worth taking. The only other piece of advice was to avoid Air France like the plague. For the Eastern European lads, life was a little more difficult and required them to get a train into Germany or Austria. Once there, they could hire a car and would then have to bribe the Polish or Hungarian border guards with US Dollars. But once over the border, it was just a question of repeating the procedure depending on how far they wanted to go. And there were certainly Russian and Ukrainian Legionnaires who managed to spend all of their leaves at home.

With the crates packed away and our personal kit loaded onto the plane, we moved out of the barracks and spent the final night in a hanger. We were confined to barracks and to ensure that we didn't wander, we'd only been left with our standard issue sports kit. The rest of our clothes were on the plane, but as an added incentive, anyone caught out on town would not be going on leave. The trouble was that even with these restrictions, the temptation for one last night out was too much to resist for some of the lads.

Andy was from Northern Ireland and had spent a few nights out with us at 'Chez Tantine'. After a few beers he suddenly announced that he was going over the wall and promptly disappeared behind the hanger. Under other circumstances we all might have been tempted to follow him, but no one else was prepared to run the risk of losing their leave. And so after another couple of drinks I headed off to bed.

'Hey....Hey....wake up will ya....'

I could feel my shoulder being shoved and opening my eyes it was still dark.

'Hey....are you awake....?'

'What?....Is that you Andy?....What time is it?'

'Look....never mind that....Have you got a spare sports kit with you?'

My head was still fuzzy and I didn't really understand his question at first, but within a few seconds my eyes started to adjust to the light and my brain began to function.

'Andy....why haven't you got any clothes on?'

'Look have you got a spare sports kit or not?'

'No I haven't. But I think Jean's got some shorts!'

He shot off in search of Jean, but still being half asleep, I thought nothing of it and went back to sleep.

Waking up the next morning I started to wonder what had happened the previous night. Looking over towards Andy's bed I could see that it was empty and so wandered over to Tom who was busy getting dressed.

'Where's Andy?'

'Probably at breakfast….let's go see if we can find him'

Andy had apparently done the rounds last night asking everyone he dared to wake up for spare clothing. He had indeed gone to 'Chez Tantine' and on the way back had been stopped by a group of locals. But instead of attacking him with machetes, they had robbed him of his clothes and left him naked in the street. He'd managed to get back into camp undetected, but with everyone's spare clothes on the plane, getting back to the hanger was the least of his worries.

Walking over to the canteen we saw Andy on his way back and he looked like the campest Legionnaire we'd ever seen. He'd managed to barrow some shorts off Jean, except that Jean was about five foot five and no more than eight or nine stone. He looked like a featherweight boxer and contrasted Andy's six and a half foot frame. The shorts could not have been any tighter and looked more like swimming trunks. He'd also robbed a pair of trainers that had been left outside one of the French Regulars' barracks, but again in his haste he hadn't noticed that they must have belonged to a midget and they were forcing him to take little short steps. The other thing that he'd also lost was his sense of humour and he told us to 'FUCK OFF' before we'd even opened our mouths. Not that this stopped us taking the piss. After all, it wasn't like he was going to run after us. Well….not in those trainers anyway.

In many ways it was a fitting end to our tour of Gabon. We'd had some great times and superb laughs. Andy got away with his makeshift sports kit and apart from the odd knowing stare from some of the Sergeants, no one asked too many questions. I think that everyone, irrespective of their rank was looking forward to leave and couldn't be bothered with him, so his only punishment was an uncomfortable journey home and a constant barrage of sarcastic comments.

After a couple of heart-stopping moments at customs I got home for leave and spent a wonderful time with my family and friends. Not unsurprisingly nothing much back home had changed, and I don't know why I ever thought it would have. Having been away so long and having seen so much it's easy to think that every-thing should have changed, but if I'd thought about it properly, I would have realised that the only thing that had really changed was me. And in some ways the fact that home life ticked along as normal was reassuring and comforting.

The first few days after leave were difficult, not least because I realised that I still had three and a half years left which was more than twice the time I'd already served. Don't get me wrong I liked the Legion, but there were times when it seemed like a never-ending slog. And once back in Calvi the platoon returned to its normal routine, with Cowhead banging Legionnaires' heads together and more than the occasional night spent scrubbing the floors. But as we neared Christmas, people started to leave the platoon for various reasons and we also received quite a few new replacements, and every time this happened, everyone stepped up another rung in the pecking order. The Milan Platoon was not where I wanted to be though and within a few months I already had my eye on my next adventure.

It had been a great time with the Milan platoon, but with people coming and going after Gabon it felt like a good time to leave.

A year after our return from Africa Jim came to the end of his five-year contract and decided to leave. He returned home to Ireland and after a few months working as a supermarket security guard applied to join the Royal Marines. Soldiering was in his blood and at the time of writing he has left the Commandos and is currently working for a private security company in Iraq. Six months after Jim left, Si also finished his contract and followed Jim into the Royal Marines where he is still serving today.

Tom met a girl and decided that the Legion and relationships didn't mix. With just over two years' service he went on leave and never came back. I've not heard from him since.

Over the next few years drink slowly got the better of Fino and ended up consuming all of his wages. On one of his many nights on town his luck finally ran out when he was attacked by a group of Corsicans in a bar. A broken bottle was shoved into his eye and he lost much of his sight. I saw him one last time in Aubagne when I was being demobbed, because he was spending time at the Military Hospital in Marseille. They were reconstructing his eye and he was over the moon to meet up with an old friend. It was sad to see him in such a state and I always like to remember him as 'Hugh Heffner,' sitting in that restaurant in Gabon with girls either side of him and a bottle of champagne on ice.

Ducs signed on again and went to Castel to become a training instructor, where, so we heard, he used to tell stories to the new recruits of how he single-handedly took on the whole of the Congolese Rebel army in order to rescue French civilians

Alf, our brilliantly determined team leader left the Legion in 2000 and went back to civilian life where I am sure he is incredibly successful. Buchy and Didier signed on again and are probably still serving, having risen through the ranks.

Six months after returning from Gabon, I volunteered for the regiment's reconnaissance platoon and did well enough on the course to be accepted. I spent my remaining three years there and had some excellent times doing everything from hunting French secret service agents during their training, to marching down the Champs-Elysees on Bastille day, as well as managing to fit in another overseas tour. I also passed the four-month medics course and qualified as the platoon's medic. In 2001, with my contract finished I made my way to Aubagne, where on a crisp February morning I found myself once again standing in the Tomb of Capitaine Danjou, waiting for the General to enter the room. Looking around at the other twenty Legionnaires I didn't recognise anyone. Some of the people I'd joined up with I could account for, but as for the others they had either deserted or signed on again.

The General talked for a short while about brotherhood.... family....hard times....and a special bond between Legionnaires. He told us that whether we'd hated every minute of our service or loved every minute of it, by completing our contracts we had served with courage. And that whatever we did in the future, to take the things we'd learnt in the Legion with us.

Only a month after leaving the Legion, I'd landed a good job and was busy buying a home with my girlfriend. From the outside it looked like a great life and for a few months it was. But I found it increasingly hard to adjust to life as a civilian so soon after leaving the Legion, and my personal life began to fall apart. After spending five years in such an intense enclosed bubble, I was impossible to live with and certain aspects of my behaviour were just weird. Even though I was living with my girlfriend in our own home, I would only ever unpack what I needed that day. The rest was in bags so that I could go at a moment's notice. This I thought was perfectly normal and I even used to unpack my toothbrush and razor each morning and then put them back in my bag. But this was how I'd lived for five years and I guess that making the change to civilian life required a bit more effort than just taking the uniform off. And with behaviour like this the inevitable happened.

It took me a couple more years to get my head screwed back on properly, and I suppose it's something that wouldn't be unfamiliar to many soldiers. But I don't regret a single day in the Legion. I hadn't really known what to expect from it when I'd stood outside those gates in Aubagne. I'd only known that I was looking for an adventure. And whatever else....it didn't disappoint.

LaVergne, TN USA
28 June 2010
187643LV00002B/133/A